WELCOME TO CONSENT

First US edition 2023
First published by Hardie Grant Egmont (Australia) 2021

Library of Congress Catalog Card Number 2022908717
ISBN 978-1-5362-2617-1 (hardcover)
ISBN 978-1-5362-3053-6 (paperback)

22 23 24 25 26 27 LEO 10 9 8 7 6 5 4 3 2 1

Printed in Heshan, Guangdong, China

This book was typeset in Nexa Slab.
The illustrations were created digitally.

Walker Books US
a division of
Candlewick Press
99 Dover Street
Somerville, Massachusetts 02144

www.walkerbooksus.com

WELCOME 🔓 TO CONSENT

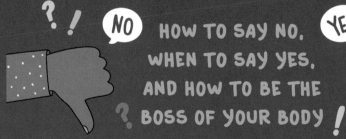

NO HOW TO SAY NO,
WHEN TO SAY YES,
AND HOW TO BE THE
BOSS OF YOUR BODY **YES** !

YUMI STYNES & DR. MELISSA KANG

WALKER BOOKS

Welcome TO Consent

We're so glad you're here. WELCOME!

Guess what?

Consent is a concept *everyone* needs to understand. It applies to situations that occur every day, to everyone.

Consent is an agreement between people that they want to do something. We tend to think that consent happens when people want to touch or get close or physically intimate with someone. But even when you're not doing those things, you *still* need to know about consent.

It matters when you agree to get a haircut, let the doctor check your blood pressure, hug your friend, or lift up a child. And it isn't always communicated with a clear "Yes, you can" or "No, you can't." Communication can also happen through body language and assumptions, among other things.

Giving consent means knowing what you're OK with and what you're not OK with—and being confident enough to communicate it clearly. It's making sure that anytime anyone asks to do something with your body, you understand that you have the right to say yes or no. And it's equally important that you understand how to treat others—by asking for their consent, and by listening to and respecting their answers.

So you'd think the rules for consent would be simple. *Yes means yes* and *no means no*—right? Well, not always. There are tons of things that make it confusing—inexperience, desire, power dynamics, poor communication skills, shyness, embarrassment, and more. Even puberty can get in the way. It's a lot!

WE DECIDED TO WRITE A BOOK UNPACKING HOW ALL THESE THINGS AFFECT CONSENT, SO THAT YOU CAN FEEL MORE CONFIDENT NAVIGATING IT AS YOU GET OLDER.

Mostly this book focuses on how consent works in daily life, but there's a section at the end about alcohol, sharing stuff online, and, of course, kissing and sex! You may not need that section just yet. That's totally OK. If you're like us, you might be *dying to know* what it says about kissing and touching—and that's totally OK, too! All parts of this book will be waiting for you when you're ready.

To be clear: there are many things beyond your control. A book *cannot* make you immune to the bad behavior of other people. But it is going to help you set your *own* boundaries. You're the whole boss of your whole body . . . and to be a boss, you need a user's manual. (Spoiler alert: this is it.)

So how do you communicate about consent? Don't worry. We are going to help you understand this new language, give you some new ways of communicating, and open you up to how cool it can be to have the tools to say yes, no, and everything in between. And we're going to start *really* simple: with a T-shirt.

Let's go!

Yumi and *Dr. Melissa* xx

Contents

FOR WHEN YOU ARE READY

THE GOLDEN RULES OF CONSENT

Consent *can* be very simple: it's an agreement between people, or permission for something to happen.

"Yes, you can borrow my T-shirt!" you say to a friend.

That sounds pretty straightforward, right? But what if you didn't know that your friend was planning to take your T-shirt to summer camp—dirty, gross summer camp? What if you said your brother could borrow it that one time, but now he thinks it's OK to borrow your T-shirt *anytime*—without asking first? And wait, what if the person asking is a *teacher*?

Consent is about more than just saying yes or no. So here are some *golden rules about consent*—using a T-shirt as an example—that are good for keeps!

Consent needs to be COMMUNICATED

You've got to *say* it, to the best of your ability. Communicate! "Yes, you can borrow my T-shirt!" Out loud is best, with a clear yes or no, but there are also other ways to make yourself clear.

Consent needs to be SPECIFIC

You can't consent unless you know what you're consenting *to*. "Yes, you can borrow my T-shirt tomorrow" doesn't mean you're lending it forever. If you didn't know about the dirty summer camp, then you didn't have enough information to fully consent. And saying yes doesn't mean you're lending your favorite pair of shorts at the same time. Unless you specifically say so!

Consent can CHANGE

You can change your mind! And it doesn't matter *why* you change your mind—you might have no reason, you might get new information (like they're taking it mud-wrestling—noooo!), or you might see your friend treating your T-shirt in a way you don't like.

And even if you agreed to lend your T-shirt once, you can still change your mind.

Actually, no!

I suppose so . . .

Consent should be ENTHUSIASTIC and FREELY GIVEN

You should feel happy and comfortable lending someone your T-shirt, and not like you've been coerced or tricked into doing it against your will. You can't give consent when you're half-asleep, for example! If you're clutching your T-shirt to your chest with big scared eyes and shaking your head while saying yes in a tiny voice, then your consent has not been enthusiastically or freely given.

POWER matters

We'll go into this more on page 96, but it's much harder to give real consent if the person wanting to borrow your T-shirt is in a position of authority over you—whether that's official authority (like a teacher, doctor, or police officer) or social authority (the most popular person in your class).

Ideally they would recognize that their position makes it harder for you to give real consent, but sometimes they won't. So you need to know how to protect yourself—and your T-shirt— in a situation like this!

Consent can be easy . . . or not

Consent happens in everyday situations where you might not even think about it—like when a friend suggests you both go hang out at their house after school and you agree. Or—yes!—when someone is borrowing a T-shirt.

But at other times, it can be more stressful, like: "Ooooh. They want my consent for a kiss. This feels so serious." Or "Eek! I don't know how to say no to this! I need to *withhold* consent."

Sometimes it will feel weird to be so up-front about consent, especially if a situation is unfamiliar or new. But that *doesn't* mean you have to do whatever is asked of you.

Sometimes your body gives out signals that things feel weird. You might breathe a bit faster or have a tiny, uncomfortable knot in your stomach. This book will help you learn to pay attention to those signals, and trust in them—because they're telling you something important!

Sticking up for yourself is important, too. So we'll help you learn to step through the weird feelings and connect with your true wants and needs. We'll talk a lot more about listening to that inner voice and looking out for those signs.

Remember, when it comes to your own body, you are always in charge.

Consent is a two-way street

Sometimes you're the one asking to borrow a T-shirt and other times you're the one lending it. The rules are the same regardless!

WHAT'S AWESOME ABOUT CONSENT?

The best thing about making an effort to discuss consent with someone is that you both know what's going on! You leave the guesswork behind. If you are clear about what you're allowing someone to do—or what they're allowing you to do—then no one has to wonder anymore.

You ask. And they answer!

They ask. And you answer!

When you say yes—or someone says yes to you—it should feel *good*. It means you both want to share an experience, experiment together, or do something fun together. It means you know *for sure* the other person is into the same thing you are—whether it's ordering hot fries with gravy or kissing!

When it's right, you just kind of feel warm and comforted.
Mel Kettle

It's kind of like driving. You never want to be in autopilot mode. You want to be in active mode—looking for those tells. Actively asking if that person is comfortable.
Luke, 17

Sometimes *no* is even more beautiful than *yes*, even though we tend to think we should always be aiming to hear a yes answer.

No—or nonconsent—is beautiful because it means the person communicating this has shown you where their boundaries are. They have done it in such a clear way that they trust you can understand and accept their refusal.

By saying no, they have created an understanding between you that maybe wasn't there before.

It's one thing to ask a question and then act like either answer to the question (yes or no) would be OK—it's another thing to be able to enthusiastically hear the word *no*. We don't lean into rejection very often. *Nevo Zisin*

I respect it when people offer to help and also are respectful of my choice to decline their offer of help. The key here is to offer the disabled person a choice instead of telling them you are doing it. *Nicole Lee*

WHY IS IT HARD TO TALK ABOUT CONSENT?

Gulp! Good question. Here are some of the reasons it's hard to talk about consent:

Society and culture

A lot of people—across cultures and nationalities—equate the topic of consent solely with the topic of sex, without realizing consent applies to many other situations as well. They may feel shame around sex and intimacy, and therefore feel awkward when it comes to talking about consent. When enough people feel this way, the society we grow up in can give off the vibe that we are supposed to feel awkward about it, too.

This is not everybody, but it could be your parents, your grandparents, or your peers. They may feel embarrassed. They may assume everyone has the same beliefs as they do. Or, importantly, they may find it hard to talk about consent because *they don't know the answers to your questions.* Perhaps they weren't really taught about consent, making it hard for them to teach you!

When it comes to conversations about boundaries, consent, and sex, there can be a lot of fear. Some adults worry that talking about sex will make teenagers go out and do it! (This is a myth, BTW—research shows the opposite to be true.) Being open about intimacy might not sit comfortably with your family's beliefs or religion.

But just because clear consent communication makes *them* feel weird, doesn't mean *you* need to feel weird about it, too. After all, consent isn't just about sex—it's part of daily life! If you've never discussed consent before, it might feel strange because it's a new (and sometimes tricky) topic. That's OK—we're here to help!

You might feel that "you should just know" what people want, or that "you'll figure it out" when you're trying to understand the boundaries of someone you care about. The problem with this is that when you guess, you sometimes guess wrong.

You might be used to putting *your* needs first, and not have much practice at putting someone else's needs first. (Can't you just assume that it's the same as what *you* want? Um . . . No! Because they might want something different.)

And here's where it gets really confusing: sometimes we're not actually sure what *we* want, either! So how are we supposed to figure it out, let alone talk about it, if we're unsure?

Some of us need help figuring out what we want and don't want. For instance, do you *want* to watch that scary movie with all your friends, even though you know it will keep you awake all night? Should you go on a date with someone who likes you, even if you're unsure of your feelings for them? We need to be able to say "I'm not sure." A lot of us need to learn new ways to say no. A lot of us need to learn how to *hear* the word *no*—and respect it. We also need to learn how to understand what *yes* means in different situations. And— this is really important—we also need to learn that it's OK to change our minds. We'll cover all of that in this book.

The feels are distracting me!

Consent can be hard to talk about because it involves ideas that make us feel awkward, embarrassed, threatened, or exposed. For instance, someone might say, "I'm having pretty strong feelings for you. Can we talk about it?" They have asked for your consent to have a personal conversation, but you may still *feel* like you want to run away screaming!

We suggest that you put up a little antenna for feelings such as shame and fear—try to notice when you're feeling them, and think about why. Feelings like embarrassment can be contagious—and passed from friend to friend or from parent to child! The good news is, the more you have these conversations, the easier and less awkward they get, and the better you get at acknowledging your feelings and moving on.

Being blunt can be scary. But it's better than avoiding the truth! *Yumi*

Because I'm a teenager!

Consent can be tricky when you're young because there are rules and expectations around what we do with our bodies, but we aren't full adults yet. People expect us to fit in and do the right thing without granting us the same power that a grown-up has.

At my school there's a boy who doesn't want to do swimming because he's embarrassed about his body. So he lies and says he forgets his swimsuit, and every week the teacher gives him a detention and calls his parents. And it's always this big drama. Everyone in the class feels sorry for him because it's a situation that can't be stopped, and we can't help him. *Dee Dee, 16*

Worrying about what your friends are thinking or doing can nudge you toward making choices that you might not like. And being inexperienced may make you a little scared and overwhelmed when it comes to sticking up for yourself. It can also push you toward pressuring someone else into doing something they don't really want to do, just because you want to try it. Consent works both ways.

REMEMBER!

IT'S NOT JUST YOU! TALKING ABOUT CONSENT IS TRICKY FOR EVERYONE. IN THIS BOOK WE'LL RUN THROUGH LOTS OF SCENARIOS WHERE CONSENT CAN BE COMMUNICATED, AND GIVE YOU LOTS OF TOOLS AND EXAMPLES.

HOW DO I ACTUALLY TALK ABOUT CONSENT?

GOOD QUESTION! THE BEST WAY TO GIVE AND RECEIVE CONSENT IS TO JUST START TALKING ABOUT IT—EVEN IF YOU'RE NERVOUS ABOUT THE EXACT WORDS TO USE.

We communicate so often in day-to-day life that we take it for granted. Whether it's asking to borrow a pen at school, glaring at your brother for being rude, or choosing lunch in the cafeteria, we're pretty good at talking and using body language to make ourselves clear. In fact, we're giving and receiving consent all the time, and we don't even think about it! But when it comes to our bodies and intimacy, learning to communicate around consent can take practice. Learning how to ask, being ready to hear the answer (whatever it is), and saying yes or no yourself are all big skills.

So if thinking about all this is new to you, where do you start? Whether it's in person, over text, or online, you start here: Ask. Listen. Observe.

Regardless of whether it's the first time or the eightieth time, anything that involves sharing an intimate physical experience—in person or online—needs consent. And the quickest way to figure out if you have consent is to actually ask. The other person or people involved should ask you, too. Here are a few ways to ask for consent:

Hey, is this OK?

Should we stop?

Do you want to keep doing this?

When you ask, make sure the other person feels safe. Be aware of your body language and *how* you're asking. And remember that giving someone the space to exit a situation by asking is a very cool thing to do. Don't forget to allow them the time to make their own decision once you've asked.

If they do want to leave, or take a breath, or just sit and chill for a minute, they can. If they don't, you can continue, and you will both feel valued and respected.

Asking is just one piece of the puzzle. But it's really important, because if there's no asking, there's no answer, just guesswork, and you (or the other people involved) might guess wrong.

Listen

Once you've asked, you have to *stop* and listen. *Really* listen. Don't leave it up to the other person to tell you to stop after you've asked. Actually pause, and make sure the answer you hear isn't just the answer you *want* to hear. If it's unclear, ask again.

MORE ON p. 21

What you're listening for is **ENTHUSIASTIC CONSENT**. You want the other person to be really into it, or at least genuinely willing to give it a try. If they say, "Yeah, yeah, just hurry up" or "Fine, whatever, I don't care," that . . . doesn't sound very enthusiastic, does it?

If your gut is telling you that the other person isn't into it, you should trust that. You can always ask again: "Are you sure? Because it doesn't seem like it, which is OK."

Remember, consent is a two-way street. If you feel like they're not telling you the truth, then *you* can decide to stop until you're sure going ahead is the right thing to do.

Observe

Observing means tuning in to the other person's body language and the way they say something.

Observing should happen the whole time during **ASK, LISTEN, OBSERVE.**

You can observe to check on whether someone might be up for something, or whether they feel comfortable when they give you an answer.

If someone is shy or afraid in a situation, they might still say they are fine to keep going. It could actually be the opposite of what they want deep down. This is where observing body language is super important to help you figure out whether someone's *yes* really is enthusiastic and freely given.

If you're in a situation where someone's *yes* doesn't sound right—it sounds forced or fake, scared or untrue— then it is a good idea to check by asking again and paying close attention to their body language. A person who looks nervous, unsure, tearful, miserable, scared, or like they are saying no with their body while saying yes with words—this person clearly needs to stop and take a minute. See also **WHAT DOES YES LOOK LIKE?** and **WHAT DOES NO LOOK LIKE?**

MORE ON pp. 19 + 24

THE WORST THAT CAN HAPPEN ISN'T THAT YOU STOP—IT'S THAT YOU KEEP GOING **AGAINST SOMEONE'S** WISHES.

Sometimes people say one thing and do the opposite. For example, I hated being tickled as a kid and always tried to push the tickler away. But because I was laughing at the same time, it didn't sound like I wanted it to stop! *Marisa, 36*

ASK ➡ LISTEN ➡ OBSERVE ➡

are parts of a cycle that keeps going for as long as it needs to. This is especially true when it comes to doing anything you're unfamiliar with or unsure about. And this is especially true when it comes to doing something intimate with someone for the first time . . . and every time!

REMEMBER

In your life, you will be on both sides of this consent conversation. Sometimes you will be saying no, and sometimes you will be the one hoping to hear a yes. Hearing or saying no doesn't make you a bad person. Both are perfectly normal exchanges when we are seeking, giving, and withholding consent.

WHAT DOES *yes* LOOK LIKE?

Yes!

A yes is a magical thing. Saying or hearing yes, knowing fully what's being agreed to, can make *yes* one of the most exciting words in the world.

Verbal consent is the best way to be sure you're getting a yes. Here are some of the ways people can say yes:

Would you please . . . ?

It feels really good when you . . .

That is great.

Let's do this!

I'd like to . . .

This is awesome. I like it.

There are also nonverbal ways to signal a yes. If someone is enjoying themselves, they may be engaged and making eye contact, or maybe laughing, smiling, chatting, and being present. Not everyone will give the same signs, though! You can ask each person what their "yes" looks like.

Yes can look like all kinds of behaviors:

* **Nodding yes**
* **Looking pleased**
* **Actively touching you back**
* **Pulling you closer**

If you're ever unsure whether the other person is happy to be doing something or whether they're definitely saying yes, the best thing to do is ask.

> I once had a sexual partner say, "You don't have to keep checking, just see how happy I am" . . . I just replied with, "Yeah, uh, I can't . . . I'm blind, remember?" *Hayden Moon*

Yes means "I agree to what has been proposed." It doesn't mean "I agree to what has been proposed and anything else that might follow."

And *yes* also means "I can change my mind anytime I want to."

> It can be harder to read visual cues because of Asperger's. I need a lot of confirmation that I'm understanding correctly. I ask a few questions. I'm, like, gullible, so I'm not very sure. *Chloe, 17*

Enthusiastic consent

> You have to take *active steps* to make sure that the other person is consenting. You can't assume that they are doing what you want them to do because they came over to your house or they slept over or whatever . . . You have to be *sure*. *Saxon Mullins*

Why does consent need to be enthusiastic? What does that even mean? Why isn't plain old consent enough?

Enthusiastic consent looks beyond words and takes into account how someone really feels about a situation, even if they're not comfortable expressing it.

Yes?

Yes!

For example, maybe you love having soy sauce on your scrambled eggs. But when you try to convince your friend to have some and he says, "Um, maybe," but looks all grossed out—that's not enthusiastic at all!

If you're the person asking for someone's consent, then look for *enthusiastic* consent. Their words and body language, and your listening and observing, will help you figure it out . . . and if you're unsure, then ask again!

And what about if someone asks to kiss you, and you feel incredibly awkward about rejecting them? Maybe you've never had to reject someone before, and you don't want to hurt their feelings. Your instincts might lead you to say reluctantly, "Uhhhhh, sure, why not . . . I guess?" even though your whole body is screaming, "Ew, no thanks!" That is not enthusiastic consent.

Intimate activities and sex are not something that you do *to* someone or *for* someone. They should be something you do *with* someone—where both of you are interacting as equals and both of you are enthusiastic about it. *Dr. Jacqui Hendriks*

Mutual yes!

There's an idea we love about consent called *mutuality*. Instead of consent being about one person asking for something and the other holding the "keys" to permission, mutuality is two people having a dialogue about what they want to do and adventuring down the path together, as equals.

We adore this idea. It could be something like, "We both decided we wanted to do more than just hold hands." Decisions are made through discussion, mutual desire, and mutual respect. This is the best situation, in our opinion!

Sexual intimacy is most powerful when both people feel safe, when both people really *care* that the other person is OK. *Mel Ree*

WHAT DOES *no* LOOK LIKE?

You might have heard the expression "no means no" in conversations about consent. It is a way of explaining that once a person has said no, their decision must be respected.

But yes is easier to say or hear than no, especially when it comes to consent. This is because a no can seem too confrontational, too final. Research has shown that when teenagers refuse something, they rarely use the word *no*.

There are lots of ways that people can say no without using the word *no*. For instance:

I really like you but I'm tired, so I'm going to go.

I'm not feeling great about this, sorry.

I only give high fives now, Gramps.

No thanks. I don't feel like it.

Auntie, I don't want to give anyone a kiss right now. It's not just you.

Hey, can we just hang instead of doing stuff?

I'm sorry, but you can't tell me what to do.

Body language also plays a part in communicating no, and each person will have different signs. Here are some things that can mean no:

- ✦ Shaking your head
- ✦ Looking unhappy
- ✦ Being silent
- ✦ Feeling sick
- ✦ Trying to leave
- ✦ Crossing your arms
- ✦ Freezing up
- ✦ Crying

- ✦ Frowning
- ✦ Appearing to look around for someone who isn't there
- ✦ Tensing up one's body
- ✦ Changing the subject or not replying at all
- ✦

This is why **ASK ➡ LISTEN ➡ OBSERVE ➡** is so important. You don't want to miss the signs that mean *no*.

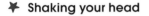

Communication during intimacy *can* be blunt and might sound like this:

I withdraw consent.

I like you, but I am not enjoying this particular thing.

Can I stop us here?

Do you like this? Cuz I don't.

Whoa, I don't like this.

This sucks. I'm going.

I want to stop.

By saying no you are not depriving someone of your body or your time, because it was never theirs in the first place! *Saxon Mullins*

As I've grown older, I just have to bluntly say it. I don't have any other methods other than saying, "I don't want to." *Lana, 17*

Remember, a no can also open up other options:

No, I hate gravy on fries! How about we just get our own separate fries instead?

No, I don't want to go see that horror movie. It's too scary! Can we see the adventure one instead?

I'm not a hugger, sorry. I give high fives, though!

WHY IS IT SOMETIMES HARD TO SAY NO?

No.

As a kid I wish I'd felt empowered to say no. And I wish I'd felt empowered to stick up for my body the way I would have stuck up for someone else's! I wish I had known my own discomfort was actually worth something, and that it was enough. *Sally Rugg*

Have you ever noticed that people are often reluctant to say the word *no*?

A lot of us are conditioned to be "nice." We try to be polite and accommodating to avoid saying no. We may want to please others. We think saying no will hurt someone's feelings. But actually, honesty is better for us, and for them. Better than finding out someone was pretending!

It's a possibility that I could be hurting the other person's feelings by not kissing them, but I usually explain myself, and at the end of the day, it's never OK to have your personal boundaries pushed in exchange for someone else's happiness or enjoyment. *Luke, 17*

To be clear, it's completely OK to say no if no is what you want to say! But sometimes we feel compelled to soften our message when we're withholding consent. That's fine, too, so long as you're being clear. And you don't have to explain why you're saying no. There's more on this on page 70.

Remember, consent goes both ways. Sometimes we need to be the one to hear no when someone is indirectly communicating it to us. Their message might be very soft, but if you notice that they're not *really* enthusiastic about doing something, they might be saying no. It could sound like:

Where's the bathroom?

Can we take a break for a bit?

I need some water.

I need to get home.

I dunno.

Not today.

It's getting late.

Ouch.

What time is it?

That feels weird.

> I have ADHD and autism and anxiety. These things can affect my ability to interpret body language. I need a few more cues—when I'm really tired and really done, I tend to be awful at picking up social cues. *Tans, 15*

The good news is, you actually do get better at saying no and being assertive— with practice! So think about it like a muscle that you can make strong. Practice saying no in a low-stakes environment, such as when you're with family or trusted friends:

> No, I don't like sardines!

> No, I'd rather read my book— thanks, though.

> No thanks, I don't want to play tennis this weekend.

If you feel reluctant to say no because you're scared about the consequences, or about angering the other person, this is a different thing and a real problem. That's a clear sign that you can't actually give real consent and you might be in trouble. The best thing you can do in this situation is get out, and get help as soon as you can. Turn to page 195 for more advice on this.

Consent Mantra: YOU ASKED, I ANSWERED

A USEFUL PHRASE IN CONSENT IS "YOU ASKED, I ANSWERED."

Sometimes the answer *isn't* what you want to hear or what someone else wants to hear. And it can be tempting to nag until you get the response you want. For example, if you refuse to lend your T-shirt, your friend might say,

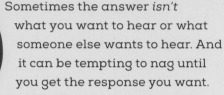

PLEEEASE, can I? Please? Why not? C'mon, you said I could last week!

No.

But she asked, and you answered. You don't have to feel bad because she didn't get what she wanted. In fact, you should feel good that you set a boundary and stuck to it. Well done, you!

WHAT IF I DON'T KNOW WHAT I WANT?

Sometimes we really don't know *what* we want. And that's OK. Often we just need a bit of time to sit with the question and let our brain mull over the answer.

Am I liking this?

Does it make me feel good?

Does this make me feel weird?

Am I worried?

Do I have someone I can call for help?

Is this new for me?

Am I excited about trying this?

Am I nervous?

Do I feel like I can be honest?

Being able to admit that you're not sure about something is a sign of maturity, and it's really important when it comes to consent. The key thing is to express out loud that *you aren't sure*.

Saying "I'm not sure" or "I don't know" is perfectly OK. It is something grown-ups say all the time.

You could also say:

TO BE HONEST, I CAN'T TELL IF I LIKE THIS OR NOT.

Let me think about it.

ARE YOU OK? BECAUSE I'M NOT SURE THAT I AM.

Something about this is making me feel weird.

Can we slow down for a sec? I just need to take a breather.

CAN WE CHANGE THE PACE? I FEEL LIKE I WANT TO JUST GO FOR A WALK OR SOMETHING.

In a romantic or intimate situation, saying "I'm not sure whether I am into this" is truthful. It's different from saying "stop" or "I don't like you." And you're allowed to take a few moments (or hours, or days, or weeks—however long you need) to figure out what is the right next step for you.

Remember, everyone is figuring out what they like and don't like—and being unsure is normal. It's just part of the process.

I think it's really important that from a young age you learn what that "Spidey sense" in your gut is—and that you're taught to trust it and talk about it with somebody that you trust. *Mel Kettle*

CAN I CHANGE MY MIND?

100 PERCENT YOU CAN!

At any time, consent is reversible—whether you're with someone face-to-face or talking to them online. It's so important to emphasize this, because for a long time people felt that once they said yes, or even *implied* a yes, there was no going back.

But that's not true. Got it? Good!

YOU CAN TAKE BACK YOUR YES WHENEVER YOU FEEL LIKE IT.

YES

Consent needs to be ongoing because in the course of an intimate encounter with another person, what you're doing with them will change. You may go from kissing to holding hands. You may go from holding hands to cuddling. They may nuzzle your neck or caress the skin on your arms. They may put their hand on your knee. Some of these things may be great for you. And some may be too much! So consent needs to move around just as your actions move around.

I explain that I have low vision and therefore I will need them to ask if something's OK when they start anything new and I'll respond to that. *Hayden Moon*

I forewarn them that I am allowed to change my mind. And so are you. It's always OK to say "I'm not feeling it anymore." *Kera, 18*

All young people should know that they can change their mind at any time. Just because you've done something with someone before does not mean you have to do it again. You don't have to keep doing something because you're worried about upsetting someone. *Dr. Jacqui Hendriks*

LETTER TO DR. MELISSA

66 I was making out with a boy from a different school, and halfway through, the smell of his breath just started making me feel sick and I stopped kissing him and said I felt sick, which was true. Is there something wrong with me? **99**

There's nothing wrong with you. You decided you didn't want to do something, and you got yourself out of it! Good job.

There are many ways to reverse consent. Here are some examples:

Let's do something else.

Hey, I've changed my mind. I want to go home.

I really like you, but I'm not up for this right now.

This isn't how I pictured it. Let's stop.

Hang on, I need to take a breather.

I said yes to kissing but not to anything else. If you're happy to stick with just kissing, then we can keep going. Otherwise, we should stop.

I suddenly feel sick! I have to go.

Please stop. I don't like that.

Whoa! No, this isn't for me. I've changed my mind.

Don't do that.

I'm not enjoying this anymore.

I feel weird about this and want to stop.

Hey, something has come over me—I need to get out of here.

This isn't what I want.

It can take courage to speak out, so sometimes it's good to have a script prepared—phrases like "That doesn't feel so good" or "Can we take a break?" or "I just need to stop things here." *Professor Catharine Lumby*

Is it ever too late?

No. It's never too late to change your mind.

Don't be worried about upsetting someone by saying no. You're allowed to be clear in your answers! *Saxon Mullins*

You can absolutely take back consent at any time—whether you've already started or are close to "finishing" any kind of intimate activity.

It could be dancing. It could be a long hug. You could be making out with someone and then decide that you don't want to do it anymore. And, yes, it can be having sex. It honestly doesn't matter whether you said yes before or how far things have gone—you don't owe the other person anything. The activity doesn't even have to feel bad—you can just decide that you're not into it anymore or that you want to change things up, and all you have to do is say that.

In these instances, communication is crucial. Make it clear that you are not joking and that you want the action to stop. If you change your mind, the other person (or people) might want an explanation, and it is your choice whether to give one. Read more in EXPLAIN YOURSELF, OR DON'T!

MORE ON p. 70

PUBERTY CHANGES EVERYTHING

LETTER TO DR. MELISSA

" I am twelve years old, and I am a bit concerned and scared. I feel like I am maturing really fast—you see, I already have hair on my vulva, I am an AA bra size, and I have to wear deodorant and bring it to school on PE days. I feel really self-conscious and I feel like I am the only twelve-year-old girl like this. **"**

With all this change, it's understandable to feel as though your body is completely out of control. And you are *definitely* not the only twelve-year-old like this! I get a lot of similar questions, which tells me that while everyone is going through the same stuff, it's really hard to talk about. At least half your class is in the same boat! So why do you feel like the only one? Well, some of it is because feeling self-conscious is also a natural—and temporary— change we go through in puberty. (Go figure—nature does all these things to our bodies *and* makes us feel too awkward to talk about it!) It's also because some topics are harder for anyone to talk about, including adults. When everyone is quiet about something, it becomes taboo, and taboos add to that feeling of awkwardness or being scared.

You probably already know that puberty changes your body. But did you know it also changes how you think and feel about things—AND what you're likely to consent or not consent to?

Puberty kicks off because of a massive boost in some of our hormone levels. What's a hormone? It's a chemical made by special tissues in our bodies called glands; there are more than fifty types of hormones in the human body. Each one is a "messenger" that travels through your bloodstream with a specific instruction to tissue somewhere in your body. For instance, "Yo! Grow hair now!"'

The girl who wrote the letter on the previous page has several different hormones whizzing around her body telling pubic hair and breast tissue to grow and armpit sweat glands to activate. Puberty hormones are pretty busy at this time in our lives. They also help change the way our brains think, how we use our imaginations, and how we make decisions!

Let's talk about some of the other big changes in puberty, too.

Physical growth spurt

In its first year of life, a human baby triples its birth weight. But did you know that puberty is the SECOND-FASTEST GROWTH PERIOD, after that first year of life? Not only do you grow in height and weight, but your shape changes dramatically. Children who were once skinny little sticks might be surprised to become curvy and soft, or stack on muscle, or both. Increases in bone size, body fat, and muscle as we go through puberty help make us the size and shape we will be as adults.

Sexual development means that suddenly—usually within a couple of years or so—bodies start to release eggs or produce sperm.

Mood swings

Your **brain** is rapidly changing, so the way you think and feel is different. You might experience mood swings that come out of nowhere! "Why am I so happy?" "Why do I feel like the whole entire world is hopeless?" These swings feel intense, from heart-clutching sadness to wild, giddy happiness and everything in between.

Our brains develop immensely—in pretty cool ways. We get new abilities to solve problems in our heads and think about the *reasons* for things. We get better at empathizing—figuring out what our grandma, little brother, or a friend is thinking and feeling. We were not able to think that way before puberty, so we've made huge leaps in empathy and smarts.

Questioning authority

Questioning some of the things that adults—especially parents—tell you is part of that higher-level thinking that your brain is now capable of. It's designed to help you eventually become more independent and able to work out problems for yourself.

Risk-taking

Wanting to do stuff that feels a bit risky or dangerous is common during your teen years. This doesn't have to be anything extreme—it might be trying out a new sport and being less afraid to fail. Or maybe it's bending a school rule—like challenging a dress code or a teacher's ideas. And it can be something that was once too scary to contemplate—like asking someone out, posting something personal online with someone you like, or making out with someone.

Wondering what other people think about you, and even *thinking* that they are thinking about you, can be an almost constant preoccupation. Concern about presenting yourself in a certain way on social media or in front of your friends can get intense as you get older.

Lots of likes on your feed can feel like a huge validation, while getting likes from your elderly relatives might actually become . . . irritating! There's a reshuffling of the hierarchy of people you care about—and friends become more important. The way you relate to people—your family, friends, teachers, parents, and other adults—can change, and you start to see the world differently.

Horniness

Feeling horny (sexually aroused) is definitely part of puberty for many people. These feelings can come from specific triggers, like seeing a sex scene on TV, brushing past the person you have a crush on at school, or imagining kissing someone. But they can also come for *no reason whatsoever*. It's just part of the messy package that is puberty, and it's your body's way of getting you prepared to think about having sex in real life.

Making decisions based on what your friends or peers are doing is part of how you carve out your identity separate from your parents/caregivers. Sometimes your peers even seem to make decisions for you (see "Georgia's Story," page 73). Figuring out what your feelings and thoughts are—separate from the influence of others—can be tricky. Because you now care more about your friends than you ever did before, peer pressure can be a mighty force.

MORE ON p. 111

Figuring out your personal values

Puberty is a time when you might start to think about the morals that have supported you through life. Sometimes teenagers question their parents' ideas or the religion they grew up with. It might be short-lived, or not.

Reassessing the world around you, questioning authority, having new experiences on your own, and learning how to make decisions—these all mix into a kind of fuel that nourishes your conscience. You start to figure out what you believe is right and wrong. Values can change throughout your life, but the teenage years give a major boost to forming your own set of ethical ideals.

All these changes have an impact on consent.

The big stew of puberty means you care more about what other people think and are more likely to take risks and rebel—which can influence your thinking and cloud your decision-making.

You are now wading into new territory—and all these unknowns mean that you don't have the backup of experience to help you.

It's not all bad, though! Even if you're not conscious of it, you now have the mental capacity to understand how something you do might affect someone else. This means you are learning how to show respect and consideration. This thinking makes you a more caring (and therefore better) friend, a better person, and even a better potential partner for someone.

MORE ON p. 52

IF I'M THE BOSS OF MY BODY, WHY DO PEOPLE KEEP TELLING ME WHAT TO DO WITH IT?

I'M THE BOSS!

Your body is like its own country. There is no outside governing body. You are its president, prime minister, boss, and CEO. **YAY!**

This applies to everybody—able-bodied, disabled, male, female, nonbinary, trans, gay, bi, straight, asexual, young, old, tall, short, from any and every racial and cultural group—*everybody*. Some people may require assistance in managing their bodies, but that does not mean they are not the boss of it. This is called **bodily autonomy**.

However, while you're still underage, your parents, caregivers, and others *do* want some say over what happens to your body. They may tell you to shower. They may chase you down the street insisting you put on warmer clothes!

In some situations they legally have to grant permission for you to do something with your body, like if you're under eighteen and want a tattoo. In rare circumstances, like major medical procedures or emergencies, there might need to be a negotiation or an override, for example, by a doctor.

Your school might require you to wear a uniform to class. A sports coach or dance teacher may want to advise you on physical exercises to optimize your performance. A doctor will want to help you take care of your body to overcome illness or manage disability. And religious leaders often want to have a say in what you choose to do with your body based on your faith.

It's important to remember that while those people *do* come from a place of authority, the final choice in what happens to your body is yours.

Sometimes you need help figuring out what to say to remind people that you're in charge. That's what this book is for.

My wheelchair is part of my body. People don't always understand this, and it's something I wish everyone knew. Do not touch, push, or move someone's chair without asking or being asked to do so! *Nicole Lee*

It's so simple, but I would now say, "My body belongs to me!" It didn't belong to other teenage boys, it wasn't the property of older men looking at me. My body didn't exist for other people; it was for me, and I would tell myself now, "You're the boss of this thing!" *Sally Rugg*

When do your parents stop being the boss of your body?

Short answer: roughly between the ages of twelve and eighteen.

Long answer: it's less about *when* and more about *how*. Your parents stop being the boss of your body through a process of conversations and negotiations as you get older. A lot of the time you won't even realize that you're talking about bodily autonomy. You might be asking to wax your eyebrows, or to buy some clothes that are different from what you'd normally wear, or to eat something specific for dinner because you're craving spicy food or you've stopped eating red meat. These are all ways you can express your bodily autonomy.

As you go through puberty, you start having a lot more opinions on what you want to happen to your body, even if they go against your parents' beliefs. It's super normal.

You might clash with your parents over some issues, and that's normal, too. Your parents are used to looking after you and keeping you warm, fed, and healthy. They remember you being tiny and helpless.

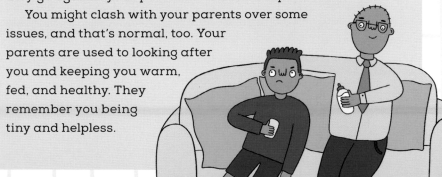

It might be weird for them to learn to give up control, and it will take some getting used to.

Hopefully, you will be able to find a middle ground where you can agree on most things—and this will gradually turn into complete autonomy. *Eventually!*

As a twelve- to thirteen-year-old I became incredibly self-conscious about what I looked like. I remember going to a tennis lesson at thirteen and wearing jeans, and my mother said, "You have to wear that short skirt!" and I said, "No way!" and we ended up having this huge fight about it. *Mel Kettle*

When I was a teenager, my dad was super strict and never let me wear a swimsuit without a T-shirt over the top or tank tops in the summer. It was partly a cultural thing, because he grew up Catholic in the Philippines, but I grew up in Australia and I hated it. *Marisa, 36*

Bosses in training

Everybody—including newborn babies—should be treated with respect.

Physically, little kids need help getting their diapers changed, feeding, cleaning, and dressing themselves. Because they are smaller and weaker and have much less power than adults, there are laws that protect children from being harmed by others.

So while little ones need adults to physically care for them, we can still show respect for them by always asking before we do things to their bodies. For example, you can ask a little baby if they'd like to be picked up before you pick them up (even if they can't respond yet), or ask a toddler if they'd like a hug before you put your arms around them. If you think about it, that's probably what you'd want if you were a tiny person surrounded by giants!

Once a child can talk or communicate with some clarity, and can manage bodily functions on their own, such as going to the bathroom (around the age of three or four), they are better able to exercise their bodily autonomy. This means they can *literally* have a say about what happens to their bodies: "Yes, I'll hug you!" or "No, I won't sit on your lap."

NO!

Respect

You probably know what it feels like when you are being respected. People show respect by caring about you—your physical safety, emotional needs, and feelings. They treat you like you matter.

When adults treat you with respect, you feel safe and visible. When people at school treat you with respect, you feel like you can trust them, even if it's just to look after your lunch while you go to the bathroom!

Self-respect means you care about your own needs and dignity. You're kind to yourself. Your feelings and preferences matter, and you are the only boss when it comes to your body.

What we do with our bodies, and what we ask others to do, is closely linked with respect—for ourselves and for others.

Respect is important for any relationship between two people—a parent and child, two best friends, a teacher and student, or a romantic couple. It translates to caring behavior. It means you consider each other to be worthy and deserving of kindness.

When it comes to consent, respect is a no-brainer. Respect is what carries us through all the steps necessary for consent to be given and received.

Consent and bodily autonomy

Bodily autonomy and consent go together like the moon and stars, sun and sky, yin and yang. In giving and receiving consent, each person is in charge of their own body, and the other person knows and respects that.

You may want to touch someone you really like. Or you may have intense and horny feelings toward a person's body. They may feel the same way about you. But that other person is always the boss of their own body, and you are always the boss of yours.

In the same way, being someone's boyfriend or girlfriend or partner does not make them the boss of your body, nor does it make you the boss of theirs. It does not give them the right to have a say over what you do with your body—what you wear, eat, or do, sexually or otherwise. Each person is still the boss of their body no matter how in love they are, no matter how committed they are to another person.

This is just as true if you're sharing something to do with your body online—any intimate activity relating to your body requires your permission, and you retain the right to say no, no matter what your relationship is with the other person.

MORE ON p. 179

Following rules and showing consideration

Sometimes people tell us what to do because we might be causing harm to ourselves or other people. This is different from them being unreasonable or bossing us around.

It could be out of genuine concern for your safety, especially if you're into stuff that can be physically dangerous, like jumping out of trees, restricting your diet, or driving too fast. People want to stop you from hurting yourself or someone else, and for this reason they will tell you what to do with your body.

Sometimes the law steps in and makes a rule about bodies that applies to everyone— like that you have to wear a mask during a pandemic, or that punching people is illegal.

People also sometimes tell you what to do with your body because if you're behaving inconsiderately, it affects others. For example, jumping up and down and having a great time at a concert may mean bumping into smaller people, even hurting them—and you may not realize it. Or someone may shout at you, "Don't walk three people wide on the sidewalk!"—because you haven't realized that doing so impacts the ability of others to share the space.

Sometimes agreeing to requests to do something with your body may seem annoying, and it may mean you have less fun. But if you stop and think about how agreeing (or disagreeing) will affect others, you may find such requests are fair and reasonable.

SOMETIMES WE HAVE TO CONSENT TO DOING SOMETHING A BIT BORING (IF IT DOESN'T ACTUALLY HURT OR BOTHER US) . . . BECAUSE IT'S THE **RIGHT** THING TO DO.

PUBERTY, BODILY AUTONOMY, AND TOUCH

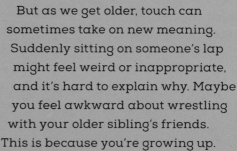

One of the effects of puberty is that we become interested in intimate contact with others. We might look for new ways to physically interact with people.

Touch is something most humans can't live without. A lot of the time, this touch is platonic (meaning not sexual—only friendly) and just makes us happy. Like if you have your arm around your friend or you're giving your baby sister a cuddle—this touch is most often sweet and affectionate and kind. Maybe you love it when your mom brushes your hair. Maybe it's the satisfying slap of a high five.

But as we get older, touch can sometimes take on new meaning. Suddenly sitting on someone's lap might feel weird or inappropriate, and it's hard to explain why. Maybe you feel awkward about wrestling with your older sibling's friends. This is because you're growing up.

My disability makes my speech hard to understand, and the easiest and most efficient way to communicate is to get my mom to translate my speech. But sometimes she needs to step back a bit so I can tell it in my own words. *Stella, 21*

This is the perfect time to start thinking about consent and touch—being aware of what it feels like when you are touched and how other people might feel when you touch them.

When you're lucky enough to be touched by a person you like, remember that you are not giving up your bodily autonomy. You're still the boss of your body. This should only be happening because you want it to. This should be happening because you consented.

And when you are touching someone else and enjoying it, their bodily autonomy doesn't disappear. They are still the boss of their body and captain of their ship. They can call "stop" or "time-out" anytime they want. They might also move away, and that's OK.

The teenage me thinks he doesn't want hugs from his mom anymore! Physical affection from my family occasionally *does* make me feel uncomfortable. *Luke, 17*

When you don't want to be touched

You don't actually need a *reason* for not wanting someone to touch you.

There are many forms of unwanted casual contact, like a stranger brushing past you or a shop assistant grabbing your elbow. It doesn't have to be overtly sexual or violent— or even touching a private body part. Someone could be touching your arm or ear in a way that makes you feel uncomfortable, and it's your right to stop it.

It also doesn't matter what that person's intent is. In other words, they might say they're just brushing some dust off your shoulder. But that doesn't matter. If you don't like it, you can tell them to stop.

A strange man tried to touch me at the bus stop. He was asking me directions, and as I leaned in to look at his map he put his arm around me. I said, "Don't touch me," and moved away. The man looked at me with big, offended eyes, like, "Whoa!"—like I was psycho and had just done something really wild. His reaction was not my problem. In fact it made me want to laugh because—what? He's offended because *his* touch was unwelcome? I was happy I'd defended my bodily autonomy. *Yumi*

A common way to avoid unwanted touch is to move out of reach. Most people understand that with this gesture you are saying no. You can also say in a loud voice "Please don't touch me" or "What are you doing?" which will draw attention to *their* odd behavior. You don't owe anyone anything when it comes to your body.

DON'T DO THAT!

I don't like people touching my waist. I don't know why! I just don't like it. And I don't like people touching my neck.
Kera, 18

UNEQUAL TREATMENT

You might know this already: There are some people in society who think it's OK to make rules about what happens to some *specific* bodies but not all. That is actually an example of discrimination, but often it's disguised as "caring" or "expectations."

It might be, "They're allowed to wear short shorts, but you're not."

Or, "It's cute if he shouts during the football game, but not when she does it."

This discrimination happens disproportionately to people of marginalized genders, to people from racial and ethnic minorities, to people with disabilities, and to members of the LGBTQ+ community. Attitudes are slowly changing, but you will definitely find that there can be different expectations around bodies and consent depending on your gender, physical abilities, sexuality, and race.

> Muslim women are commented on by everyone from white supremacists and racists, who say, "Take that off"—about the hijab—to conservative Muslims, who say, "This is how you're meant to be wearing it!"
> *Amna Hassan*

Sometimes strangers will come up and pat my head (because I use a wheelchair). This happens more often from people who talk to me like I'm a two-year-old. They speak to me like I'm not cognitively aware or "with it." *Stella, 21*

All over the world, girls and women are told what they can and can't do with their bodies. And these "rules" and expectations do *not* apply to boys and men in the same circumstances. This includes how many babies women are allowed to have or if they should have them at all, how women must dress, or how loudly they can speak. Rigid beauty expectations and some fairly narrow ideas about what a "nice" girl can and can't do give people the idea that they can tell girls what to do with their bodies.

Intersect this with a disability and/or being part of a racial minority, and the result can be a profound disrespect for a person's bodily autonomy.

I am literally going about my business, and men on the street who don't know me say, "Give us a smile!" *Dee Dee, 16*

I'm fat. People feel like they can just touch me—they will touch my belly and say, "Oooh, you've been eating well!" *Ally Garrett*

Let's be very clear about it: bodily autonomy is equally important for everyone, whatever their age, gender, race, sexuality, culture, or ability. Discrimination occurs—and it sucks. You're not imagining it. And when you have the energy, you can push back.

YOU ARE THE BOSS!

When it comes to bodily autonomy, the law says this is really clear-cut. My body, my rules.

Wow! I find that a very rude thing to say.

I'm sassy. Don't test the limits of my sass!

I think that's a pretty old-fashioned view nowadays.

PLEASE DON'T ASSUME THAT I'M ILL-INFORMED.

We obviously see things differently.

You're boring.

DIFFERENT CULTURES, DIFFERENT MEANINGS

We all have different backgrounds and come from different walks of life, so what works for one person may feel violating for another. Some people think it's OK to overlook another person's bodily autonomy simply because they come from a different culture or look different from their peers. That's a type of discrimination, and it is absolutely not OK.

WHEN IN DOUBT, DON'T TOUCH!

My brother has autism and doesn't like to be touched. When I visited I'd always give him a kiss and a squeeze, and I could see him flinch—he didn't like it. But my attitude was, "It's good for him. I'm teaching him about touch. I'm very comfortable with it so I can help him adjust." I finally realized I was inflicting my values on him. *Anonymous*

In my culture, it is very disrespectful to touch someone's head. The exception is small children and babies, who have wonderful heads that are lovely to touch. If someone touches my head, I don't like it and I will communicate this by ducking away. *Yumi*

Sometimes I find, as a female with a disability, when I say no, people don't respect my boundaries. *Jacqueline Greene*

They walk up to me and say "I love your hair"—and put their hand in my hair immediately! That's the first meeting—a complete stranger, feeling like they can put their hands on me. I feel like an animal in a zoo. My hair is very black, Pacific Island Afro, with a lot of volume. It looks like a traditional Afro that just stands up. I love it! But honestly sometimes I feel like I have to tie it up because I can't deal with other people's energy. *Mel Ree*

It's almost like disability makes you public property. It can be things like strangers putting a hand on my shoulder or a pat on the top of my head while I'm out in public rather than offering a simple handshake, or someone grabbing or blocking my chair so I can't move. I've had people squat down to talk to me and put their hand on my lap, and I wonder—would they do this to anyone else? *Nicole Lee*

I saw the hand coming toward me and I just moved my head out of the way. I said, "No. Am I a doll?" He looked confused. I said, "Have I ever asked to touch your hair?" And he said, "No, but my hair is not as amazing as yours!" And I said, "No. It's my hair, and it's not appropriate to touch it, especially without asking." *Paula Baxter*

People often comment on my skin because I'm Asian. It makes me uncomfortable. I still get a lot of comments about my ethnicity. *Anouk, 18*

I grew up in a small town in Malaysia, and my mom had bright orange hair and the whitest skin. Strangers would come up in the street and touch her skin because they had never seen anything like it. It made her really uncomfortable and didn't happen in her Sydney suburb, where lots of redheads roamed the streets. *Dr. Melissa*

HOW TO SET YOUR BOUNDARIES

Setting a boundary is a way of saying, "This is a line I don't want you to cross." Boundaries are where saying yes and no sets limits.

Boundaries are different from bodily autonomy because they change as we get older. For instance, little kids have no problem running around naked, but (most) older people definitely have a boundary around doing that!

WHEN WE'RE TALKING ABOUT BOUNDARIES AND CONSENT, WE MEAN PERSONAL PHYSICAL BOUNDARIES AS WELL AS ETHICAL, EMOTIONAL, AND MENTAL BOUNDARIES.

Sticking up for your boundaries—and sometimes explaining them—is part of how you get people to treat you the way you want to be treated.

It's really common for teens to want more personal space and privacy from parents and family members—so you might set up boundaries that are partly physical and partly mental. For example, you might not want your parents bursting into your room, so you ask them to always knock first and not go in when you're not there.

You might not want your little sister or brother going through your phone—not because you're hiding something, but just because it's your phone. There's a boundary there. You might have boundaries around how much you share online or offline about your period, learning to shave, crushes, pimples, or bathroom habits—anything that feels personal. Boundaries are also about our morals and values, which can take time to figure out. Examples might be *I never steal* or *I think it's rude to make fun of people who are different, so I never do.*

It takes practice to set a boundary. You may start by slamming doors, shouting, or throwing tantrums—that's how you express that someone in your family has crossed the line. But as you get a bit of experience, you get better at calmly explaining your boundaries.

Don't say the N-word around me. Don't hate on Asian people around me. I won't stand for it. *Anouk, 18*

What are your boundaries?

Before you can explain or defend your own boundaries, you need to know what they are. And it can be hard to decide what you will consent to in the moment! Sometimes you feel pressured by friends, or by FOMO, or the fun of the situation. Sometimes a split-second decision means you do something that you *never* would have agreed to if you'd had a chance to think it through.

It's good to figure out boundaries when they're *not* being tested. A good time is when you're feeling calm and have time to think on your own.

Here are some ideas to get you thinking about your boundaries, with no right or wrong opinions. Thinking them through privately can help you figure out where your boundaries lie. You can also make up your own scenarios.

I would never make fun of a homeless person because I know each and every one of them has their own personal story of why they are homeless.
Jacqueline Greene

66

- I don't want to kiss someone unless we know and like each other.

- I don't want to see anyone naked.

- I don't want to be seen naked.

- I only hug friends and immediate family.

- I won't flirt with someone online who I don't know in real life.

- I am up for kissing.

- I won't post negative comments about someone's weight, no matter who they are.

- I am happy to do more than kissing if I love the person.

- I don't want to have any kind of sex until I've finished school.

- If I can't tell my mom about it, I don't want to do it.

Having clear thoughts around these ideas helps you to make the right decisions in the heat of the moment, and helps you to stick up for yourself if someone is trying to pressure you to move your boundaries.

Don't forget that your responses will change over time. Check in with yourself. We're often influenced by what our friends are doing and how much experience they have—but even with these influences, usually we have a good idea of what feels right for us.

When your boundaries change

As you get older, the adults around you might not realize that your boundaries are changing. You might not feel comfortable doing something that you once did!

66 My three best friends in elementary school and I were inseparable. We had had so many sleepovers and spent lots of time together outside of school. It had been like that since second grade. I distinctly remember this sudden change in me, I think it was fifth or sixth grade. We'd been to the pool for a swim and my friend's mother told us all to have a shower together to save water. The other three immediately stripped off and jumped into the shower. I really, really didn't want to. I didn't want to take my clothes off, even though we'd all had showers and baths together for years. Suddenly I wanted privacy. I was in a complete panic. I couldn't figure out how to say no. 99 *Hannah*

Hannah's boundaries had changed. Because this was new to her, she had real trouble explaining! (Fair enough, too.) Here are some things Hannah could have said:

★ "Whoa! I suddenly feel really weird about being naked in front of everyone. I'll just shower on my own later, thanks."

★ "Hey, I am having an attack of shy feelings. I won't shower today. Or I'll shower by myself, if that's OK."

★ "I know we used to do this all the time and I feel embarrassed to say this, but I am not comfortable getting naked in front of everyone anymore! OK?"

★ "Guys, I have an announcement! I no longer do public nudity!"

★ "No thanks. I don't want to."

★ Changing the subject or not replying at all.

Like Hannah, you might realize that there's a new boundary around something you never even thought much about before. You might say no to something that previously was perfectly OK. And similarly, you might end up doing things or saying yes to something you *never* would have done before!

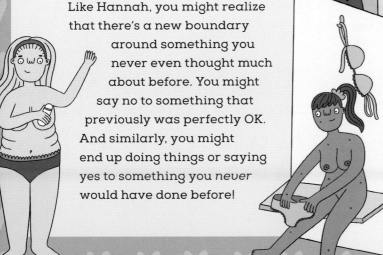

EXPLAIN YOURSELF, OR DON'T!

I often got asked for hugs by strangers at music festivals. At first I said yes because I didn't want to be rude. I thought being friendly was part of my job as a music reporter. But I realized that saying yes meant I got covered in their sweat and body odor, which stank and grossed me out. Sometimes they would hold on too long. I realized I actually hated it. Setting a boundary meant I always replied with a hard no—always. It never felt like it was negotiable because everyone got the same answer: no. *Yumi*

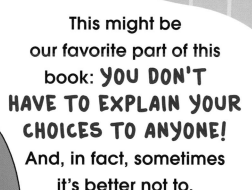

This might be our favorite part of this book: **YOU DON'T HAVE TO EXPLAIN YOUR CHOICES TO ANYONE!** And, in fact, sometimes it's better not to.

1 Sometimes your inner moral compass is saying no. You don't know why. And your inner compass doesn't give much detail! You might not be able to explain how you feel, so don't.

2 Having a reason gives a person something to argue with. For example, if you say, "I don't want to go with you because I don't feel safe," they might reply, "Oh, you're safe! Look, the pathway is well lit and I know CPR. You're *so* safe." Explaining why you don't want to do something can weaken your initial *no* statement. Just saying "I don't want to" is actually enough.

When you say no, some people say, "Well, actually . . ."—and want to argue with you! It's annoying. Teenagers get underestimated. *Tans, 15*

SELF-AWARENESS = FEELING + THINKING BEFORE ACTING

Consent and self-awareness

Consent is often thought of as being about an *action*: you agree to *do* something. Or you don't. But almost every physical action is intricately linked to feelings—and sometimes we need to slow down and pay attention to our feelings to know what they are.

This is called self-awareness: being conscious of your feelings *and* understanding how those feelings change the way you think and behave.

You might have had a teacher or a parent say, "Think before you act!" Actually, what often needs to happen is more like, "Be aware of your feelings, *then* think, *then* act."

FEELING

THINKING

ACTING

CONSENT WORKS BEST WHEN ALL PARTS OF SELF-AWARENESS ARE PRESENT.

But sometimes connecting with our feelings isn't easy.

GEORGIA'S STORY

In sixth grade I had my first crush. But kids in my class decided who you got paired up with—it wasn't me and my crush! I remember feeling embarrassed being told, "You go with him," and that was that. We didn't do anything, but we were a "pair." It was fun but confusing. My body was also changing; it was exciting and awkward. There was so much going on.

Inside feelings vs. outside pressure

Feelings and thoughts almost always go together. When our feelings are intense or we feel pressured to do something, we often let those feelings guide our actions. We tend to not stop and check our body's reactions, reflect, or think about what's going on—pressure can "short-circuit" our brains and persuade us to do something without thinking much!

MORE ON p. 111

Feeling worried about what others think of us can negatively influence our decision-making. Believing "I need to do this to make them happy" or "They'll like me more if I agree to do this thing" can override the feeling of "Yuck!" or "I don't like this." (Being a teenager can be really intense!)

In these moments, try to make an effort to get in touch with yourself. Ask yourself, "Do I really want this? Will doing this make me happy, or am I scared, showing off, or trying to fit in?"

Remember, only *you* know the answers!

It's even harder if you've never been in a certain situation before. Especially when feelings and thoughts contradict each other.

In Georgia's case, she thought, *I feel excited to be part of this* and *I don't want to pretend I actually like him* simultaneously—because both of these things were true!

Georgia told us her fear of being seen as weird, coupled with excitement at being included, meant that she wanted the experience and didn't want it at the same time.

Being able to recognize your feelings in the face of pressure, excitement, and fear is a skill you need to learn.

So how do I know what to do?

This is where the thinking part kicks in.

Some people like to make actual lists of pros and cons. Others just weigh the positives and negatives in their minds. The key thing is to think it through all the way to potential consequences. That will help you decide what's right for you.

And if you're panicking, it's OK to say, "Hang on, I just need a minute to think." (*Impulsivity*—a word commonly used when teenagers make reckless decisions—occurs when you skip the thinking process altogether!)

This last thinking step also involves remembering to check in with your values, what you *want*, and being respectful of yourself and the other people involved. Here are some prompts for the next time you need help sorting through your feelings:

ENTHUSIASTIC

EXCITED

WORRIED

CERTAIN

RIGHT NOW I FEEL . . .

CURIOUS

PRESSURED

UNCERTAIN

SOMETHING ELSE?

Have I considered the feelings of others?

Am I clearheaded (sober)?

Is what I'm agreeing to clear and specific to me?

Is it a free choice?

Do I know what's involved?

WHAT'S NEXT?

Am I enthusiastic about doing it?

Am I safe? Should I do anything to make sure I'm safe?

Can I change my mind?

Are there parts of this I want to do but parts I don't want to do?

Is everyone happy to be involved and consenting?

Can the other person freely change their mind?

Georgia went along with being paired up with the boy she didn't particularly like or dislike. She says now it wasn't a decision she made but believes that, fortunately, the consequences weren't devastating. There was no other contact with the boy, other than being in the same classroom.

Georgia also says now, as a young adult, that she wishes she'd understood the relationship between feelings, thoughts, and behaviors when she was younger.

Experimenting with the way we act is part of the teenage experience. We don't always get it right and—truth be told—we make mistakes. Quite a lot. But so long as we do our best to avoid hurting others, and hurting ourselves, that's usually OK.

Once we've been through the feeling, and had a chance to think about it, then the last step in the process is deciding how to act. Sometimes we make mistakes repeatedly before figuring out how to correctly interpret our feelings and our thoughts and then—victory!—make the best choice for ourselves about how to behave.

Between the ages of about fourteen and seventeen, I was madly trying to figure out what was "wrong" with me. I knew that I was different from my friends. It turned out that I was gay! I didn't understand who I was, and I think most teenagers are still trying to figure out who they are and who they could fall in love with. During this age I think I was seeking out sexual connections with teenage boys because I felt like there was a piece of the puzzle missing with me. So I was seeking out that sexual contact to see—*Maybe this will work for me? Maybe it will feel different this time?* None of those experiences were nonconsensual, but I feel like I wasn't fully informed, because I didn't understand that it would be OK to actually not want sexual contact with boys. I didn't really understand what I was searching for. *Sally Rugg*

WHAT IT MEANS TO FEEL SAFE

When it comes to consent, the feeling of being safe is so, so important.

Safety is basically the condition of feeling free from danger, risk, and injury. Feeling safe is a prerequisite for consent, just like being awake is!

But safety isn't just a neutral feeling. It's also about feeling good, secure, and able to try something new and knowing that even if it doesn't work out or you don't like it, you'll still be OK.

We went rappelling when we were thirteen. It was totally scary, but the guides were supportive. They let us take our time. Some girls got to the clifftop and just couldn't go down. They froze or cried. The guides were pretty cool about helping when we needed it and letting us figure out some stuff as we went. *Yumi*

You'll notice that being able to trust someone makes you feel safer than you might have otherwise felt. It also means you know they won't judge you, whatever you decide. Maybe that will sway you toward trying out other new things, or maybe it won't. It's up to you. But that "safe" feeling is something to keep in mind when talking about consent.

I was with a "sort of" girlfriend and she wanted to take a photo of me, and she said, "I want you to make this cute, sexy face!" And I was like, "Uhhhh! I dunno!" And she was like, "Please!" And I was like, "I don't know!" And then, she was pushing it a bit: "C'mon! I won't show anyone!" It didn't make me happy. It didn't make me feel like we had a close relationship. *Tans, 15*

Trust your gut

Sometimes a situation makes us jittery, uncomfortable, or scared—in a word, we feel unsafe. Sometimes it just doesn't feel right. Even fully grown adults sometimes have trouble explaining why they are feeling a certain way—they just know it's wrong. That's OK.

You might get a racing heart, sweaty palms, a queasy tummy, a tingling sensation in your extremities, or weakness in the knees. You might want to lash out and run away. Some kids feel quite angry and can get violent and aggressive . . . It's just your body telling you that you're not happy about something.
Dr. Jacqui Hendriks

HEY! LISTEN TO ME!

These gut instincts are really powerful. They are how our bodies tell us something before our minds have had a chance to process it.

You don't have to have a perfect explanation for *why* you're feeling uncomfortable. You just have to trust that you are, and that's enough of a reason to remove yourself from the situation.

Some of the most important things to keep returning to when gauging your own consent are the questions of *Does this feel right?* and *Am I happy about this?*

If your answer is no, then it is your right to remove yourself from what's going on, call for a time-out, or say, "No thanks." And remember, you don't have to explain why you're saying no.

MORE ON p. 70

Once in a while you do get that unconscious gut feeling, "This is a *bad* idea. We shouldn't be doing this." *Luke, 17*

I think for us to stand our ground and know our boundaries, we really have to tune in to our gut. There's a lot of emphasis placed on rationality and logic and being able to explain why you want something to happen or not happen. You need to turn down the volume on what other people are saying and turn the volume up on what your gut is telling you. *Amna Hassan*

"Stranger danger" upgrade

We learned a lot about stranger danger in elementary school, like, every year. It's stuck in our memories. In high school we learn more about safety in relationships, like with our friends or if we're dating. It's a big topic. *Ruby, 15*

Everyone we interviewed for this book remembered "stranger danger" from when they were little. The message was basically that if a stranger was being creepy, you should tell an adult you trust as soon as possible. And everyone agreed this was a sensible, valuable message.

Fast-forward to now, and the world is a little more complicated. For a start, pretty much everyone is online, chatting with friends, making new ones, and often interacting with lots of strangers. You can have an entire social life built from people your parents and peers don't personally know.

Second, many teenagers are now thinking about new kinds of relationships and intimacies that their parents might never have experienced, so it can be hard to seek advice about what to do. Online flirting and hookups are common and can feel a bit exciting and a bit dangerous.

Your own internal safety meter is a useful guide in navigating consent and stranger danger in the new world.

> Sometimes people I know start having a relationship with someone they meet online—they're friends of friends on social media, like Instagram or Snapchat. Not total strangers, but you haven't actually met them. And they start flirting or sharing personal stuff, like they are in a relationship, but they never see them in person. And I think that can be a bit unsafe. I don't know how consent works in a situation like that. *Aimee, 15*

With online intimacy, there's a lot of potential for being tricked or lied to. If the person you're talking to doesn't have any friends or family in your real-life social circle, it's difficult to verify that they are who they say they are.

Growing up with smartphones and laptops means being online is natural for you. But that *doesn't* mean you shouldn't be careful. Just as you'd have a conversation about consent in real life, you should talk about consent before you take things any further online. And while you may not consent to something you've shared being spread around, you don't know that you can trust a stranger to respect that. They are unverified.

One of the key ways people get in trouble on the internet is by doing things impulsively—without thinking them through. So don't write, share, or send something that might be hurtful, degrading, or offensive (including things about *yourself*) unless you've really weighed the possible consequences.

You need a safety network

In elementary school, when we were quite little, school taught us to "tell your parents" if someone touched you when they shouldn't. About stranger danger. But what if you don't want to talk to your parents anymore? *Moya, 13*

Every young person should have a safety network: three to five adults that they know and trust. At least one of the adults needs to come from outside your family, and for them to qualify, you need to be able to tell them anything and feel confident that they will believe you.

Sometimes it may be easier to talk to someone who's *not* your mom or dad, like an older cousin or sibling, or a teacher at school.

Safety network

If you're reading this and thinking, "I don't have a safety network outside of my parents," *now* might be a good time to think about who you could add—and let them know. You can be really blunt about it and ask them: "Hey, everything's OK right now, but do you think I could call you if I was in trouble but too scared to tell Mom?"

Some good candidates could be:

- ★ your mom's or dad's best friend
- ✳ the parent of a close friend
- ✦ your aunt, uncle, or a non-blood relative who fills that role
- ✳ a counselor or therapist
- ✦ your doctor
- ★ a favorite neighbor
- ✦ a teacher

When each of my kids reached high school I gave them a small laminated piece of cardboard for their wallets that had the phone numbers of different adults that they trusted. Grandparents, aunts, uncles, family friends. It was old-school, since they have all these contacts in their phones now, but it was nice to hand them something tangible that said, "These adults will look out for you, too. You matter to them." *Dr. Madison*

IN CASE OF EMERGENCY

· Jenny ·

Emergency Contacts...

- · Mom
- · Dad
- · Georgia

BEST TEACHER EVER

DAD

#1 COUSIN

MOM

BFF'S DAD

PRIVACY SETTINGS

Privacy is the right to keep your personal matters to yourself and not share them publicly if you don't want to. Other people should get your consent to share something that you might want to keep private, and vice versa.

There's a whole range of different personal settings for privacy. Some people are happy sharing pretty much *everything*. They'll post pictures of their families, their report cards, their food, their dates, their hairy chests, *everything*. Or at school, some people will be very quiet about what they did on the weekend while others will talk loudly about every detail in front of everyone!

Where you sit on this spectrum is personal to you. You can change where you sit and how comfortable you are to share. And you can actively consent—or choose not to consent—to how your experiences and information are shared among other people online or in real life.

But it's important to remember that your privacy can be lost, stolen, or given away without you even realizing it. So when you're sharing something personal, it's always worth making sure that you're genuinely prepared for it to not be private in the future. If you're not, hold it back. You can always choose to share it later, if and when you're ready.

In our age group, if you do share that you've kissed someone, or whatever, there's a possibility that that's going to get shared, and spread. *Drishti, 14*

It's not always easy to respect someone's boundaries. Sometimes I've divulged a secret—said something that I probably shouldn't have. *Luke, 17*

DON'T TELL A SOUL!

THIS WILL BE A LAUGH!

TELL THE WORLD

ONLINE PRIVACY IS JUST AS IMPORTANT AS IRL.

Maybe you and your friends normally tag one another or share pics or posts without thinking or because you all assume that no one will mind. It's still worth regularly checking in with one another. You don't need a reason to say, "Should I always ask before I post a picture of you? Do you want to be tagged?" or "When we're chatting, can you promise that no one else is listening in or reading our messages?"

How to talk about privacy

When you want someone to keep something private, there's a big difference between mentioning that they shouldn't share it and *asking* them not to share it.
Picture this:

1 A good friend tells you something personal. As she's walking away to get to class, she calls out across the hall, "Hey, just keep that between us."

2 A good friend tells you something personal. Then at the end she says, "Look at me. Listen. What I just told you is super personal. It's really important that it stays between you and me. Do you understand?"

You say, "Sure, sure!"

Then your friend looks you in the eye and says, "Hey. I'm serious. You *really* can't tell anyone."

The second time feels a lot more serious, right? And you're much more likely to remember it.

The thing is, sometimes we forget what's OK to share and what's not. But you're much more likely to remember someone's privacy settings when they use careful verbal communication as well as body language to emphasize the importance of their request.

You don't have to do this every time you share something personal. But if you really don't want something to be passed on, it's worth making sure the other person knows how you feel.

People always say, "Yo, don't screenshot. Yo, don't show anyone." Of course there's always cases of people not respecting that, but most of the time people are pretty good. *Anouk, 18*

Secrecy vs. privacy

I was a very private kid. I didn't tell any of my friends when I got my period. And I didn't tell the person I had a crush on that I used to think about them all the time even though the crush lasted three whole years. That's OK. Those were my secrets to keep private. *Yumi*

One time I was with my friend at a shop and they stole a magazine for the code in it. Then they told me after, when we got home, and told me not to tell anyone. So I didn't tell (until now, of course). Keeping the secret made me feel really guilty about it, almost as if I had committed the crime as well. *Noodles, 15*

There's a big difference between secrecy and privacy. Privacy is usually about protecting personal information that may be embarrassing or that you just don't wish to share. Secrets can sometimes protect risky or even criminal behavior.

In sexual assault cases the pattern that we often see is a younger girl with an older guy who's not much older but already driving, and he will pick her up from school, so she's already doing something she's not meant to be doing. Or he takes her to a party she's not meant to be at. Or illicit substances are involved. So that's often conflated with the assault, and the girl is more reluctant to disclose. *Dr. Ellie Freedman*

When someone else asks you to keep a secret, it can feel weird, and that could be because it's not right. Remember to trust your gut, because weird feelings can be an early warning sign. They might even be making you complicit in something you don't want to be part of. We're not talking about innocent secrets here, like that they forgot to put underpants on after gym. We're talking about situations that ring alarm bells—like if the person asking you to keep a secret is older than you. Or they're in a position of power over you (like a teacher or a religious leader). Or the person would get in real trouble if the secret were public knowledge. These are all signs that you should tell someone what's going on, because the secret isn't serving you. It's serving them.

If something doesn't feel right, it's worth asking yourself some questions:

★ **Why do they want you to keep a secret?**

✷ **Whom does the secret protect?**

★ **Does keeping the secret make you more safe or less safe? How does it affect their safety?**

✷ **And when they say things like, "This is our secret," are they trying to make you take ownership of something that is wrong?**

One way to stay safe is to have some older people in your life you can tell everything to. Talking to someone about things that might feel weird or inexplicably shameful is really helpful, because together you can figure out why things are making you uncomfortable and whether you need to do something about it.

Hey, can I talk to you about something?

MORE ON p. 85

The secrecy bottom line

Sometimes it's OK to keep a secret (like when it's a good surprise for someone else). Other times, keeping a secret can be harmful—for you or others.

There would regularly be questions to my health column, Dolly Doctor, from teens who were worried about a friend or sibling. It was when they found out or were told something that made them really worried for the other person's safety, such as feeling suicidal, going into a spiral of some sort, starving or harming themselves, or revealing something very traumatic—which was often about consent being absent.

It took a lot of courage for these young people to ask for help. The person they were worried about was someone who had entrusted them with secrets and private thoughts. In all of these examples, my advice was consistent—there is a "secrecy bottom line," meaning there are some things you are willing to keep secret and some things you are not, because they endanger people. It's important to figure out when that bottom line has been crossed. Dr. Melissa

A bottom line can be:

★ someone's life is in danger, such as being suicidal

✦ someone has been abused or assaulted

✦ someone is becoming more and more unwell and refusing help—such as spiraling into depression, losing lots of weight due to an eating disorder, or not taking vital meds for a health problem

The secrecy bottom line is often enshrined in law in cases when people are at risk.

MORE ON p. 160

It's always a good idea to talk to your friend first and tell them you are really worried. They may not give consent for you to seek help on their behalf, but you can let them know you have a bottom line that is backed up by law— and you care about them enough to risk making them angry by seeking help.

As a youth leader we were kids ourselves and sometimes had to remind kids of the dynamic between us—"I'm going to stop you for a second and let you know that I can't necessarily keep this a secret." *Nevo Zisin*

It is an act of love to spill a secret that can save someone's life. By speaking up, you could help them find ways out of an unsafe situation. To risk making someone you care about feel angry or upset in order to keep them safe is an act of courage.

HOW POWER DYNAMICS AFFECT CONSENT

You might be thinking that consent is pretty clear-cut by now: you want an enthusiastic yes, an honest no, or time to figure things out if you're not sure. Easy!

But here's another crucial element you need to consider: **power** can change *everything* about consent.

Power is the ability to influence or have control. When it's used respectfully and ethically, it can be awesome. But when power is misused, it can be devastating.

IT MATTERS BECAUSE POWER OR A LACK OF POWER CAN AFFECT A PERSON'S ABILITY TO FREELY GIVE CONSENT.

AND WHEN WE TALK ABOUT POWER DYNAMICS, WE MEAN LOOKING AT HOW MUCH POWER EACH PERSON IN AN EXCHANGE HAS.

Here are some common relationships where there is a **power imbalance**:

teacher—student

coach—team member

boss—employee

support worker—disabled client

doctor—patient

customer—retail worker

older relative—kid

religious leader—congregant

prison warden—prisoner

big, strong, muscular person—
smaller person

police officer—civilian

celebrity—fan

All of these power imbalances make consent murky. In lots of instances, the law recognizes this and puts safety measures in place so that people with more power cannot take advantage of those with less power. But sometimes it's up to us to recognize power imbalances in action and take charge ourselves to ensure that consent can still freely occur.

An itchy little example

Imagine this: a teacher says to you, in front of the whole class, "Hey, can you please come over here and scratch my back?"

That might seem a bit disgusting to you, but they're your teacher, and they have the power to give you a bad grade on your next essay. So you feel like you have to nod and say yes, and maybe you'll do it and even laugh and make a goofy face at your classmates and turn the whole thing into a bit of a joke.

It might look like you gave consent, but the power imbalance between you and your teacher means that you couldn't really say no. Or you could have, but . . . *how?* What would you say? Would you get in trouble? Would it be awkward, or damage your standing with the teacher?

So let's change the context. If a friend in your class said to you, "Hey, can you scratch my back?" it would be much easier to say no if you wanted to! This is because you're more or less equal with them. There is no power imbalance forcing you to consent.

All through high school I worked part-time in a shop and the motto was "the customer is always right." It meant they had the power. I found it hard to stick up for myself if they were bullying or being rude. *Yumi*

98

I spent a lot of time questioning how friendly I was toward him that he thought we could have a romance. There was a lot of self-recrimination from me. I blamed myself. He wasn't a manipulative power guy who was going to make my life a misery . . . but he should've known he was much more powerful than I was. *Xuân*

Being a woman in a wheelchair, there are so many places, situations, and scenarios where I feel disempowered and another person is in a position of power over me. I have to trust support workers to come into my house, help me take a shower, and help me get into bed. *Nicole Lee*

When power imbalances don't seem bad

Sometimes a person might *want* to be in a power imbalance—like a music fan and a rock star. Imagine this is you, alone with your favorite singer. OMG! If they want to kiss or touch you, it's exciting, right?

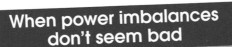

The thing is, in an intimate situation with someone who has more power than you—like, if they are a full-blown adult and you are not—they will be in charge. If they're a rock star and you're in their hotel, you are alone in a very grown-up situation. You might feel like you have fully consented, but the power dynamic will never be equal. It leaves you vulnerable to pressure, to coercion, to saying yes to things you don't want to do. It will make saying no to anything the more powerful person proposes very, very difficult.

The power imbalance can be less obvious. The most popular kid in your year has social authority that you do not have. Could you say no to them?

How do you handle a power imbalance?

If you do find yourself in a situation with a power imbalance, it is harder for you to truly give consent. So what can you do?

The first thing is to call it out. By naming it as a power imbalance, you bring it out into the open. You could say, "Wow, the power dynamic feels very lopsided here" or "This feels like a very unequal power situation." Giving something a label exposes it. Interestingly, a lot of people who are usually more powerful find it very difficult to imagine what it's like for the person who is less powerful! We get that it can be hard to call out a power imbalance in some situations, though. This is where you might turn to an adult or older person that you trust to help you out.

MORE ON p. 85

Second, check in with the legality of the situation. Is the law being broken? There are federal laws for the whole country, but laws may also vary from state to state. Just *knowing* how the law views the situation may help *you* to frame it your own way.

MORE ON p. 160

Third, take the time you need to check in with yourself. Are you OK? Are you scared, drunk, or feeling wildly out of control? Time may be what you need to get back to finding where you sit ethically with this situation. Time will allow your gut instinct to communicate.

If you are the person with less power, then you need to think about whether your rights are being respected and whether there is a way for you to leave.

Unless you are able to say no safely and without negative consequences, consent can't be freely given.

If you are in this situation as the person with more power, you need to be extra mindful of checking in and creating space for no to be said—and heard. Think about how to equalize the dynamic. It might not be possible—if not, you should walk away or hit pause.

MORE ON p. 104

When power is used for good

None of this is to say that power is always bad. There are plenty of examples when people in positions of power use it to do good things. It might be celebrities using their power to draw attention to injustice. Or your teacher calling out homophobic language from another teacher. It's the philosophy of so many superheroes, but it does happen in real life, too!

Power, gender, and consent

It takes a really long time to find your power as a young woman. Not everyone is born really assertive and aware of their individual human rights. It is harder for certain women to stand up for themselves, and their cultural background can often play a part in this, too. When you do find your voice, don't be afraid to use it, and don't hate yourself if you didn't use it straightaway. *Marihuzka*

You and your friends have probably already been exposed to common expectations about gender and consent. For example, the idea that it's OK for a boy to be pushy with a girl if he likes her, even if she tells him to stop. Or that a girl can't actively ask for what she wants by (for instance) making the first move. Or she can't forcefully say, "Go away!" because a girl should "always be polite."

These are stereotyped attitudes that have been around for a long time, and they are *so outdated* and old-fashioned 🤮. Boys *aren't* always in control. Girls *aren't* always submissive or passive. Nonbinary people are often pushed into gender roles based on their sex assigned at birth, which may not be a good fit for them. And human interactions *aren't* always heterosexual.

But some men do believe that they wield—or *should* wield—power over women and nonbinary people. And in lots of ways, women, girls, and nonbinary people have been conditioned by society to accept and go along with this. You don't have to be like that.

THE IDEA THAT A GIRL'S NONCONSENT, OR A NO, IS A WALL TO BE WORN DOWN BY A BOY USING FORCE, NAGGING, REPEATED REQUESTS, SULKING, OR THREATS TO LEAVE IS UNACCEPTABLE. IT'S JUST NOT OK.

And this equally applies to girls being pushy, and people in same-sex or nonbinary couples using coercive tactics, too. Boys can also suffer from gender expectations. They might be expected to come across as "tough" and confident when it comes to intimacy and sex. And *not* being either of those things can have repercussions—from girls and from other boys. If you see someone behaving like *no* is just an obstacle, or they're trying to bulldoze their way through a no because they think the no is negotiable, you can call them on it. Not only is that behavior sexist and rude, it's also gross and in some situations illegal.

Size and power

Even if two people are the same age and on the same level, there can sometimes be a physical power imbalance where one person is stronger and bigger than the other.

Bigger or taller people might be accustomed to towering over others, and if that's you, it's worth spending time thinking about how this power imbalance can have a real influence on a smaller person's ability to consent.

A smaller person may feel intimidated or nervous that they will be overpowered by physical force, and this might make them less likely to say no—and, as we know, *one of the most powerful elements of consent is your freedom and ability to say NO.*

> Yes is a yes, a no is a no, and a maybe is a no.
> *Michala Banas*

If you are the physically smaller person in this situation, it is important to understand that your power exists in other places—usually your words! Don't be afraid to communicate your feelings. Ask for what you want. Insist that your needs and rights be taken seriously. Be *loud* if you need to.

If you are the stronger person, it is important that you understand how to give the physically weaker person the space and the power to say no. Give them time to think through their choices. Remember that *no* is sometimes communicated through body language, through words that aren't *no*—and through silence. **BEING RESPECTFUL SHRINKS THE POWER IMBALANCE.**

Check in with them: *Are you OK? Are you feeling safe? Is there anything I can do to make you more at ease? Is this feeling cool? Do you want to stop? Do you want to try something else?*

Check in with yourself: *Am I doing everything I can to make sure they feel safe? Do they understand that I would accept and listen to them if they said no? Is there a way I can communicate that they have power, too—to ask for what they want, to slow things down, to speed things up, to call "stop" on the action, or to just walk away?*

CONSENT Challenges *and your friends*

Handling consent like a boss is a challenge! Here are some of the most common challenges that can happen with your peers—and ideas for how to deal with them.

It's just a game: truth or dare, spin the bottle

By agreeing to play games like truth or dare or spin the bottle, you are opening yourself up to a situation where you may find your boundaries being challenged. Which can totally be part of the fun! But the basic rules of consent still apply: if something happens in a game that makes you uncomfortable, puts you at risk, disrespects others, or crosses your boundaries, you can always change your mind, call a time-out, or stop. At any time.

Truth or dare

In this game the players take turns answering embarrassing questions truthfully.

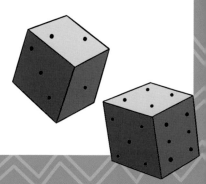

It's usually something like "Who do you have a crush on?" or "Have you ever thought one of your brother's friends was cute?"

Players can choose to do a dare—a classic is eating a dog biscuit or running up to a stranger and saying, "I love you!"

Even little kids like playing truth or dare, because the tension and silliness of it can be fun.

Remember the golden rule: if a game stops being fun for you, it's not a game anymore. You can always stop playing if things get weird. Better for everyone to roll their eyes and move on than for you to do something you'll seriously regret.

Spin the bottle

Playing spin the bottle is a rite of passage for some teenagers, and within the game itself lie a bunch of contradictions about what is considered OK and consensual and fun, and what is not. The risk is part of what makes it exciting.

In the game, you spin a bottle on the floor, and you're "supposed" to kiss whoever the bottle points to.

I was forced into playing spin the bottle as a teenager and budding homosexual. It was a little fraught for me! I was held down, and she gave me a love bite. It was horrible. *Nick Pezza*

In a lot of ways, it's a gift and a joy for daredevil teens because it gives them permission to explore kissing and intimacy with others. Maybe you'll even get to kiss someone you secretly like! But pressuring intimacy in situations where a person may feel uncomfortable is problematic.

The good news is that even if you choose to start playing, you can stop at any time. You can get up and walk away, saying, "I'm done with this game!" You can pretend to get a phone call. Or you can be the person who says, "Do you know what? I've just been reading about consent and this game is making me seriously uncomfortable. You guys enjoy—I'm going to go redo the playlist."

There were a lot of times when the bottle spun to me and I said, "Nah." And people said, "Come on, you should respect the game." I said no because usually it would be trying to create a sexual interaction where there was already an existing friendship. If you have a close friend you don't want to do that kind of thing with, it can really be damaging.
Luke, 17

When you don't see it coming

Sometimes people make decisions about what's going to happen that take you completely by surprise. The other person might assume you "get it," that you've read between the lines—and their assumptions have led to a wildly different outcome from the one you imagined.

> I was shocked out of my skin when a guy tried to kiss me at the end of the night! I thought we'd gone out together as friends. He thought it was a date. *Casey, 20*

When you don't understand what's happening, it's tempting to pretend, to seem cool, and to go along with it. But have you enthusiastically consented? When making assumptions, people can fail to seek consent. For consent to be real, it's very important that both parties understand what's being proposed.

If you don't understand, ask questions. Like "What's happening here?" It might feel dorky, but saying things out loud can be really powerful. Like "What? Is this a date? I thought we were just friends." Or at the hairdresser, "What are you doing to my hair? I didn't ask for bangs!"

Checking in with yourself, even saying out loud, "Am I OK with this?" is a good way to start or restart the consent conversation. You can check in with the other person, too: "Are you OK with us doing this?"

The thing with autism is that our brains work differently. We don't understand metaphors or anything like that. That extends to flirting. I don't get it, I really don't. So I have had experiences where someone has been suggesting something sexual and I've just had absolutely no idea. *Hayden Moon*

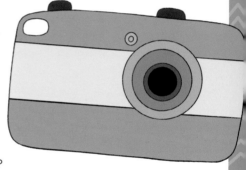

You can ask someone to be more specific. If someone is asking you to "send a pic," it's totally OK for you to ask for more information. What does that mean? Who will see it? Why do they want it? What sort of pic are they asking for?

Do they absolutely agree *not* to share it? And remember that *you* hold the power in this conversation—because *you can always decline to do something if you don't want to do it!*

If someone kisses you without asking, and you don't want it, you can push them away and say, "Don't kiss me" or "I don't want to kiss you." You can say, "What are you doing?" Say whatever you want. "Yuck! Get off me!"

If someone surprises you with a kiss and you *like* it, you can say, "Whoa! I wasn't expecting that, but I like it!"

Peer pressure

I never really had friends "pressuring" me to take a drink. If anything, for me it was more like a "pack" mentality. So there'd be a group of cool people who I'd be on the outer fringes of. If they were doing something I normally wouldn't do, I'd sometimes do it, too, in the hope of being considered to be part of the team, part of the pack. It's almost self-imposed peer pressure, like, "If I do this, maybe they will like me." *Penny*

Peer pressure is what we feel when we think our friends, teammates, colleagues, and so on want us to do something, and we feel a kind of pressure to do it in order to be liked by them. It's part of wanting to fit in and be accepted.

Anyone can feel peer pressure at any age, but it becomes intense during the teen years. You might suddenly want to try new things, take risks, win the approval of new friends, or feel closer to your existing friends.

Peer pressure can have positive effects—like maybe your friend convinces you to go for a jog when you couldn't be bothered, and you feel great afterward! But sometimes it can feel uncomfortable, coercive, or even unsafe. Peer pressure can be a mighty force working against consent.

If you're in a situation where you feel like you're being pressured to do something—laugh at a racist joke, make fun of someone different, eat or drink something you don't like, behave a certain way—it always helps to stop and take a breath. Think about:

★ Why do I want to fit in with this particular group?

✦ Is this what I want for myself?

✦ Will it make me happy?

★ Could I get hurt—or hurt someone else—by doing this?

★ Will I feel weird/sick/regretful about this tomorrow?

When it seems like *everyone* is doing something, it takes guts to go against the grain. **SOMETIMES ALL YOU NEED IS ONE FRIEND TO ALSO SAY NO.** One friend can normalize your reaction and make you feel like less of an outcast. In most situations, that friend exists—but other times *you* need to be that first person to say no. You never know who's waiting for you to speak up.

MORE ON p. 206

We were at a friend's place and I was dared to do something pretty extreme, and everyone else was encouraging me, egging me on. My best friend said, "You never have to do it. It's just a game." And then everyone stopped and went, "Of course, of course," and stopped egging on the situation. *Dee Dee, 16*

It's surprising, but a lot of the time, most people won't care if you opt out, especially if you don't make it a big deal. Sometimes you can chuck a vague excuse out there ("I hate jokes like that," "I'm allergic," or "That makes me feel sick"), but it's also fine to just say, "No thanks." If someone actually pressures you directly (which, BTW, is super uncool), you can say, "Wow, why are you making a big deal out of this?" or "Why do you care so much?" And finally: "Look, I said no. We're having a nice time; let's just drop it."

Someone was saying to my grandpa, "Why isn't she married?" And he said, "Leave her, she's on a walking stick!" It's hard to convey how funny that was in Arabic—he meant you can't rush someone who's on a walking stick. I can't tell you how important it was then to feel loved, to feel affirmed, by a family member who didn't cave to the pressure. *Amna Hassan*

The friends I've hung on to since high school are the ones who accept me when I'm sad, when I'm silly, when I'm excited and wild, or when I'm anxious. But we don't always have to do the same thing, and that suits me perfectly. *Marisa, 36*

CONSENT
Challenges and adults

At school

Outside of your family, teachers might be the adults you spend the most time with in your teen years. They can guide and inspire you. Nag you to death about homework. Make you laugh, roll your eyes at their terrible jokes, or not leave much of an impression one way or another.

But there's definitely a power dynamic at school, and teachers have the upper hand. Sometimes they want to teach us to do things for our own good, like sticking to deadlines. Or they do things for the greater good—like shushing us to protect the class's learning. Sometimes they're upholding the school rules and are therefore allowed to do things like give detention.

AT OTHER TIMES, A TEACHER MIGHT UNWITTINGLY ASK YOU TO DO THINGS WITHOUT UNDERSTANDING THAT THEY CROSS YOUR PARTICULAR BOUNDARIES.

114

> Talking about BMI or "health" in PE class feels like warfare if you're a fat kid because you hear about "tackling childhood obesity." Your body is a "problem." I got teased at school for being fat. *Ally Garrett*

Maybe your teacher doesn't understand that you have shyness when it comes to, say, being weighed in front of your classmates. Or that you feel sick about dissecting frogs in science. Maybe you feel sensitive about discussing your home situation as part of an English assignment.

In these cases, your teacher is assuming your consent, so you might need to take them aside to explain why you cannot give it. You can say things like:

I feel really uncomfortable and exposed talking about my weight in front of everyone. I know this is part of the assessment we're doing, but I would rather keep that information to myself.

This crosses an ethical boundary for me and I'm not comfortable. I'm happy to do a different piece of work instead.

I really need you to understand that my home life is private and I can't talk about certain things in front of everyone.

For good reason, there are some hard rules around what teachers can't do. They are strictly forbidden from getting romantically involved with students, or physically or verbally abusing them. They also can't do anything *close* to this—which means no flirting and no intimidation or threats to cause physical harm.

MORE ON p. 160

Sports

In this section, we use the word *coach*, but we could be talking about anyone from an athletic trainer to a sports psychologist, coach's assistant, director of athletics, department staff, or supervisor.

Coaches seem to understand what a privilege it is to work with children, and, for the most part, they're respectful of the responsibility.

For kids involved in sports, it's worth knowing that it gets more serious the older you get. While your body always belongs to just you, your team or your coach may feel like they have a say about how you optimize your body for the sake of the sport or for the team's success.

When I was in a younger sports competition or field, it was about improving our technique and participating in the game. Now it's more about getting tested, nutrition, making progress, paying attention to how you treat your body. They are respectful of your body, but they also let you know that you need to follow this training. *Drishti, 14*

Because the coach–athlete relationship can involve a degree of intimacy, sometimes the coach can overstep boundaries—either accidentally or on purpose.

One way that coaches could cross boundaries is the way that they speak to the kids—hyping them up and then criticizing them if they weren't doing their best. I didn't like the high pressure that you get from your coaches and that expectation to perform. *Corey, 17*

As with students and teachers, there is an inherent power imbalance between an athlete and a coach. And just as with teachers, the law recognizes this by making it illegal for a coach to become sexually involved with an athlete, usually one who is under eighteen. Check your state's laws and your school's or team's policies for more specific information.

At work

Your first paid job can be so cool and so fun. You're meeting new people and earning money—it's exciting! But since you're young and inexperienced, this can put you in the vulnerable position of being the weaker person in a drastic power imbalance. You may not always feel it, but you are the less powerful person in your workplace in relation to your boss, to customers, to more senior staff, and even to staff on the same level as you who've been there for longer.

Being new, I went into the control room to watch, and at the end of the show the audience got up and danced on the set with the contestants. The executive producer suggested I go down and have a dance, but I said no. He said, "Oh, Xuân, why not? I'd love to bend you over!" And all the men in the control room just laughed and laughed. *Xuân*

I had a casual job in hospitality during winter break. There was this guy who kept touching me on the butt. I told the manager, and he laughed it off. I wonder if he would have acted differently if I'd been a girl. I avoided this guy all the time after that. *Jackson, 22*

When you're overpowered and outnumbered, it's very hard to protect your boundaries and stick up for yourself. So what can you do about it?

You are entitled to a safe working environment, and your employer has a duty by law to provide this to you. This includes ensuring your working environment is free of sexual harassment. Sexual harassment laws vary from state to state, so it is valuable to know your state's laws. But it's also important to trust your gut if something doesn't feel OK. Sexual harassment can take many forms—these are just a few:

★ **sexually suggestive comments, jokes, pictures, or gifts in the workplace that make you feel offended**

✴ **unwelcome or inappropriate touching, staring or looking, sexual gestures, or indecent exposure that makes you feel intimidated**

✴ **intrusive questions about your private life or physical appearance that make you feel offended**

★ **unwanted requests or pressure to go out on dates or for sexual acts**

It's worth pointing out that not all flirting or romantic attention in the workplace is inappropriate—if you genuinely enjoy it and consent to it, and the other person is not in a position of power over you (e.g., they are not significantly older, a manager, or able to hire or fire you), then it can be OK. In fact, the workplace is where a lot of people meet their long-term partners.

I was attracted to someone I worked with—but we were on an even footing and ended up dating for, like, six months. *Abby Edwards*

The bottom line is that you have the right to feel safe at work. It's a rule enshrined by law.

If you feel you have been sexually harassed, you could tell the person directly that what they're doing is inappropriate. "It makes me feel sick/uncomfortable when you talk like that. Please stop."

Another option is to take your complaint up the chain of command. Talk to your manager, or their manager, or the owner of the business. Talk to your parents or someone in your safety network.

And if that doesn't feel safe or comfortable, you can contact your local antidiscrimination body to make a complaint. Google "Who do I talk to about sexual harassment?" to find the best organization in your area.

At the doctor

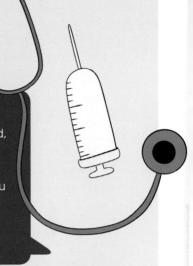

I needed my male doctor to do something that involved a vaginal examination. He said, "OK, you've got options—I can do it for you today, or you could make an appointment and I'll do it a different day, or I can refer you to a female colleague and you can go and see her." And I remember thinking, "Wow! You've given me choices!" *Mel Kettle*

Growing up with a disability meant that when I was young people didn't involve me in decisions when it came to surgery and medical procedures. I hated that. *Nicole Lee*

To take care of your health, your doctor sometimes needs to see or touch parts of your body that you don't show anyone else. But they still need your permission before they do so. They should *always* seek your consent first—ideally by asking directly, "Is it OK if I examine you? This is what I will do . . ." Sometimes they take shortcuts, like saying, "OK, show me where it hurts" or "I'll just get you to lie down on the table now . . . " Doctor's appointments usually come with the expectation that you will be examined. But that doesn't mean you can't ask questions or say no. If you're not sure about why or what the doctor needs to examine, it's your right to say, "Hang on, can you explain what you're doing first? I'm nervous." And even though they're busy and there may be a sense that they'd like to hurry things along during a consultation, you can still say, "You know what? I don't feel comfortable. I'm going to leave."

IF A DOCTOR NEEDS TO EXAMINE YOU, ESPECIALLY IF IT INVOLVES PARTIALLY UNDRESSING, YOU HAVE THE RIGHT TO HAVE SOMEONE ELSE PRESENT SUCH AS A PARENT, CAREGIVER, NURSE, OR FRIEND (EVEN IF THE DOCTOR FORGETS TO OFFER FIRST). YOU CAN ALSO REFUSE TO BE EXAMINED.

When it comes to procedures and treatments, the law says that once you're an adult, you are able to give this consent to doctors without a parent or guardian involved. But the law in some places also recognizes that adolescents younger than eighteen *may* be mature enough to give consent without a parent's or guardian's permission. (This is all to do with those incredible brain and body changes that happen during puberty—see page 38.)

For a doctor to figure out whether you can give consent without getting your parent's or guardian's permission, they may consider things like:

- ★ your age—in some states the law says you can give consent below the age of eighteen

- ★ your legal relationship with parents or caregivers—emancipated minors can give medical consent

- ★ your capacity—how able you are to think through the treatment and its consequences

- ★ your financial and home situation—a minor managing their own financial affairs or living separately from their guardians can legally give medical consent in some states

- ★ your relationship status—in some states, a minor who is married, divorced, or pregnant can give medical consent

- ★ your understanding of the procedure or treatment—a doctor should explain everything about what is involved, including different options for treatment, side effects, and benefits, and check your understanding

- ★ that your consent is voluntary and not given under pressure

- ★ that you have the right to say no or to change your mind.

In an emergency, for example, if a doctor believes it is necessary to treat you to save your life, they are usually allowed to carry out medical treatment on you without your or a parent's or guardian's consent.

With familiar adults

My uncle does this thing that really annoys me, and I don't know what to do about it. When I walk past him he smacks my ass. It's not any more than that, and he's actually very kind and funny and we get along well. I just don't know how to tell him that I hate this. *Miranda, 16*

Adults who know you well—like family members—can sometimes take liberties with your boundaries. Maybe they remember when you were a baby and say things like, "I used to change your diaper!" Or your mom says, "I'm not going to knock—I saw you naked when I gave birth to you!"

Adults need to respect your boundaries, but some of them might need a bit of practice—some reminding that you're not a baby anymore.

This particular aide had a phobia of elevators! She wouldn't let me use the elevator—and she wouldn't let another person go in the elevator with me! So I was forced, without my consent, to go in my manual wheelchair up the escalator! I felt quite powerless in the situation. I wasn't listened to. That's what upset me the most. *Stella, 21*

Here are some things you could say to protect your boundaries with adults you know:

★ If I were an adult and we didn't know each other, would you do that?

✹ That used to be OK, but I'm fourteen now, and I hope you can see that it's inappropriate.

✦ Hey, I've been learning about consent, and what you're doing is without my consent.

★ Hey, I love you, but I hate it when you do that. Can you stop?

Adults who know you well might repeatedly push these boundaries to "tease" or "have fun." Muster up your powers of good communication to let them know, through both words and body language, that you do not find it funny. If you have to, leave the room and maybe slam a door on your way out for good measure. If they still won't listen, take the problem to a trusted adult.

I used to write a letter if it was really serious. No one could argue with a letter. *Yumi*

Boundaries

We're allowed to call a family meeting. This is where my mom, stepdad, and siblings discuss serious matters—it can be anything from changing curfews to the amount of allowance. Everyone knows it's serious, so this is when I bring up the serious stuff. *Dee Dee, 16*

For when
YOU ARE
ready

Let's get into more detail about consent around sex—because this is often where we find the most confusion, shame, and fear.

From this point until page 206, we're going to talk more about the sorts of things you might encounter when you're old enough and ready for them—crushes and kisses and beyond—and how to include consent in these situations.

 We're assuming that you're more likely to be *thinking* about sex than actually having lots of it. But things like kissing, touching, sexting, or sharing stuff privately online are all part of sex and becoming sexual. All these kinds of intimacy involve feeling comfortable with your body and your boundaries. They involve trust and respect. And they all involve **consent**.

We want people of all ages to read this book, including kids—because practicing consent needs to start *way* before sex does. To make this section approachable for kids to read, we have *not* gotten too detailed with the many and various forms of sexual intimacy. To be clear: this section is *not* about how to have sex. It is about *consent*—which is a massive part of sex!

Do *you* consent to hearing real talk about consent in sex? If not, that's OK! Just stop reading now. You can come back when you're ready to read more. You might want to jump right to the end, FINDING YOUR PEOPLE (page 206), because we have an important message for everyone there. The EXPAND YOUR VOCABULARY and MORE RESOURCES sections (pages 208—211) might also have some useful information for you.

FROM CRUSHES TO KISSES

One of the special, awkward, and thrilling things about adolescence and puberty is that it can be a time for becoming sexual. There are new sensations in your body, different kinds of feelings toward other people, and new ways of seeing yourself.

Like everything about humans, there's plenty of diversity—not everyone has all these experiences. Take your time. If it happens, it'll happen when you're ready.

It might be exciting enough just to have a crush on someone without taking it any further. Or you might start interacting with other people in ways you never did before, including being physically intimate—for instance, cuddling, kissing, or holding hands—or being sexual with someone.

Wherever you are, it's good to understand how consent works when it comes to navigating crushes, kisses, and having sex in a positive and healthy way.

A beautiful lesson to learn growing up is that you're totally allowed to take the time you need to do things at your own pace. Most of my friends got their driver's licenses at eighteen—but I was in my thirties when I got mine! It took me that long to be ready, and I'm OK with that. *Yumi*

Puberty hormones change your body and also help to change the way the brain thinks and feels. Crushes, feeling "horny," falling in love, and loving a romantic partner are just a few examples. Adolescence can be an emotional adventure park—full of thrills and scares and big unknowns!

WELCOME TO CRUSH WORLD

Crushes

What is a crush? A crush is a special kind of feeling. It's liking someone *deeply*—in an intense, breathtaking, and romantic way. It's different from thinking your friend is cool or that an older kid is super smart and admirable. It's heartfelt, and sometimes "crushing"! It's a big feeling! Crushes are often caught up in fantasy—having an over-the-top, exaggerated idea about someone.

Getting a crush on someone is a good way to test out feeling your feelings. You can fantasize about your crush, have imaginary conversations, and picture your lives together without any real-life consequences. It's *fun*. And you can keep it private or share it with your friends.

In a typical crush, the other person is slightly out of reach. Maybe the age gap is just too big. Or they're your guitar teacher, or they're gay and you're straight, or for some other reason it would never happen in real life.

But can crushes crush you? There can be a fine line between a huge crush and an unhealthy obsession. If your crush is on someone you don't know, then you might be unable to function properly as you yearn for them to materialize out of your phone or TV. And if your crush is on someone you do know, and the feelings aren't returned, then it's really important to understand consent. Stalking someone is not OK—online, at school, anywhere. Making them uncomfortable is not fun. Writing their name over and over in your journal? A little bit fun.

I had a crush for ages—and ages!—on this boy in my grade. I'd get breathless around him. And then just this year he became my boyfriend. Those "wild" feelings went away. Now I'm with him because he makes me feel safe and cherished. It's different from a crush. *Anouk, 18*

Kissing

When you want to kiss someone you like and the chance arises to make it happen, your deepest wish is that they *want* to kiss you back. This is consent in action—you are consenting, and hoping that they consent! If they do, it can honestly be the most amazing, joyful thing in the world.

But how do you navigate consent in kissing, especially if you've never done it before?

At our age, we're probably up to kissing . . . Sex might have to be left until (we're) seventeen or eighteen.
Noodles, 15

I feel like anytime I do want to take it further, from, like, passionate kissing to touching private parts, he says, "No, I don't want to, I don't want to at all." He's not interested. He just can't. No way. It's fine, but is there something wrong with me or something wrong with him? *Miranda, 16*

There are lots of ways that romantic kisses can happen consensually. Some people find themselves falling toward each other spontaneously if they're caught up in the moment. Others are a bit more deliberate and ask first: "Can I kiss you?" or "Do you want to kiss?"

Asking out loud is the gold standard, but there are other ways to seek consent. You can pause and look in the other person's eyes, and even raise your eyebrows as if to say, "You up for it?" You can lean in for a kiss, but leave space so they can lean in, too—or pull away—if they want. Make sure you wait for their response before leaning in farther.

If you've already started kissing, and you realize you're not sure if the other person is OK, you can stop and ask, "Are you OK with this?" or "Do you like this?" It doesn't make it dorky or interrupt the vibe—it's just showing simple kindness, which is lovely when you're making out with someone.

MORE ON p. 149

If what you're doing changes or you start trying something new, it's good to check in with them again to make sure their consent is still active.

And if the other person doesn't want to kiss, or if you're both enjoying kissing but they don't want to take it further, that's OK. Don't push them into doing something they're not ready for— just relax and enjoy what makes you *both* feel good!

The pressure to kiss

Kissing is something you should do when you feel ready. But if you feel like peer pressure is affecting your ability to consent to kissing, you're not alone.

When I was fourteen, I had a boyfriend, and all he seemed to want was for me to kiss him. Like, a real kiss. I think his friends pressured him all the time to make sure he had done it and he had to report back to them. But my friends also pressured me. They'd ask me, "Have you kissed him yet?" and "What was it like?" I eventually kissed him and it was not great. We broke up after that. When I was sixteen and going out with my next boyfriend, I didn't want to kiss him for months. I think I was really affected by what happened when I was fourteen. *Samantha*

We all develop at different speeds. You might feel like you've got to check off every experience as quick as you can—including kissing—so you don't get left behind. This is a common feeling during teenage years. But trust us—there's no scarcity of people wanting to kiss you in your future. When you're ready, they'll be there, puckering up!

"HOW DO YOU GET GOOD AT KISSING?"

is a question we've been asked a lot. The thing with kissing is that it's pretty personal! Get good at kissing by being thoughtful and considerate with your partner, asking if they like something, if they want more pressure or less. Also think about the way you like to be kissed, and try to create that feeling. Kissing around the neck, ears, and throat can be super tingly and tickly and nice.

If you're not sure you want to kiss

It is perfectly OK to say, "I'm not sure about this. Can we start and then see if it's OK?" Some other ways to express this:

Can we go slow?

I haven't kissed lots of people. Can we not rush it?

I'm feeling a tiny bit uncomfortable and unsure. If I say "stop," make sure you listen.

Even full-grown adults with lots of experience get nervous about kissing. Be consensual with yourself; allow yourself to feel what you're feeling. If the nerves are too much, you don't have to force yourself. We promise there will be other days to kiss!

If I could give advice to younger teens, I would say go at your own pace. *Anouk, 18*

What's scarier than receiving a no is receiving a yes that isn't wholehearted. *Nevo Zisin*

FEELING HORNY

LETTER TO DR. MELISSA

> Every time I see something about sex I get horny! But it feels good! Is this common or am I just not normal?

> Hey, I'm fourteen and I get horny all the time—help!

I used to write for a teen magazine called *Dolly*. In one year, almost a quarter of the questions that came to *Dolly* magazine were about crushes. A smaller percentage were about feeling attracted to someone in a sexual way, or just plain "feeling sexy." There were lots of questions about how to kiss, and about sharing intimate messages or images online with someone you liked.

Most of the time, the writers of these questions had not had sex with anyone. They were just experiencing a completely natural sensation that they referred to as being horny. Some of the teens who wrote to the magazine were curious about feeling sexy, "hot," "turned on." Boys often asked about erections. One reader described the feeling as "twinkles down below." Over the years these questions didn't change—feeling sexy, or horny, happens to most people and is often first noticed around puberty.

These new feelings range from being pleasant to intensely good, but what I also noticed in many of the questions was a degree of anxiety. Why? Well, there are lots of reasons, but one of them, I believe, is because we aren't taught about feeling sexy—it's a kind of taboo topic, especially when you're young.

Dr. Melissa

OK, what's the deal?

So you suddenly have this incredibly nice feeling in your body. You know it's linked to sex, but you don't know exactly why or how. You're not really in control of it—and *no one wants to talk about it* . . .

So let's talk about it!

Being **horny** is a physical reaction that's also called **sexual arousal**. You don't have to be touched to feel horny—it can just happen! It might happen in a dream. Or by thinking about someone. It's your body's way of getting you to think about sex, and it's kicked off by the

flooding of hormones to the brain and body that occurs during puberty. Feeling horny is totally normal once you've gone through puberty (as is *not* feeling horny—we're all different).

Adults can feel awkward admitting that teenagers have these feelings—which is ironic because we passed through puberty, so *it happened to us, too.* It's also a private thing, and it can be embarrassing to talk about!

Puberty hormones make it possible to become horny, but lots of other things have an impact on whether we feel horny in any given situation. Our mood, past experiences, the way we feel about someone, whether we think others will judge us, or judging the situation ourselves can change our body's response. Being horny can be wonderful, and it should never get in the way of consent.

The myth about who's hornier

You might have heard the myth that boys are hornier than girls. This isn't true! I'm a doctor, and I can tell you that girls can be JUST as horny as boys. Some people may experience sexual arousal more intensely than others, some people barely at all, but this feeling does not favor one gender. *Dr. Melissa*

Even though the science is clear, the myth about boys being hornier persists. This has the effect of making some sexual feelings and experiences seem more "normal" than others, more "acceptable," and excludes whole groups of people.

So if a girl is naturally horny, she might be reluctant to admit it in case the person she likes thinks it's weird. Or she's scared she'll get trolled. If a boy doesn't feel horny at all, he might pretend otherwise in front of his friends. We hope it's clear that both scenarios are unfair!

There's definitely more of an expectation that guys are hornier and more out to have sex, whereas girls are more reserved and more "unbothered" by desire . . . but the reality is that girls can be pretty forceful about getting what they want, pretty out there, and pretty sexually oriented. *Luke, 17*

I know a lot of guys who are really shy, and they're more submissive and inexperienced and want to be considerate, and considerate of how they should be behaving in that situation. *Drishti, 14*

Horniness and consent

The thing to keep in mind is that sexual arousal can motivate you to try things that you haven't done before. That can be good if you're ready to try those things, but it's also OK if you're still not sure about it and want to sit it out.

And horniness should never be used as an excuse to pressure others—this is where consent comes in.

Let's say you're romantically involved with someone. You *really* like them—but they want to go slower than you do when it comes to exploring each other's bodies. You must respect their pace and accept that they do not consent to certain things.

It's probably helpful to know that no one has ever died from being too horny! There are ways to manage feeling horny if the person you're with doesn't want to do the things you do. You can take time out, walk away, drink a glass of water, do some deep breathing . . . *You* are in control.

In private, you can masturbate to let off steam! It's good for you and helps you learn about your body and your sexuality. It also alleviates horniness.

Porn is the worst teacher

In most porn, two people have wordless sex. There might be noises and random words being said, but people don't really *talk* in porn, and they rarely ask for or give consent. This is totally unrealistic! In the real world, sex is chatty with lots of laughter, and it often starts—and continues—with full conversations. "Do you want to have sex?" "Should we . . . ?" "May I please . . . ?"—the basic consent questions!

A lot of what's considered "mainstream" heterosexual porn includes niche activities that aren't actually very enjoyable for many people. Porn can have the effect of normalizing action that is degrading, painful, and even violent.

Let's be clear that what you see in porn is probably *not* what most people want from real-life sex. If you model what you do from what you see in porn, you're probably— sorry!—doing a bad job. Research is also telling us that kids are getting exposed to porn from as young as late elementary school. This can actually be quite scary for kids who have barely started puberty. And even if it feels a bit exciting or fun, it creates unrealistic ideas about sex, making real sex much less enjoyable.

Porn is a thing—that's an unavoidable fact. So remember that what you see is fake, often misogynistic (degrading to women), and full of people pretending to like things they might actually hate—and it doesn't teach you anything about sex. You may be better off with reading, asking people, listening, and experience.

Consent needs to be sought even for the showing of porn, and showing pornography to minors is illegal. Nonconsensually exposing others to porn is unacceptable, and in some contexts can be a form of sexual harassment.

WHAT IS SEXUAL HARASSMENT?

Sexual harassment is unwelcome conduct of a sexual nature. It includes unwelcome sexual advances, requests for sexual favors, and other verbal, nonverbal, or physical conduct of a sexual nature.
—US Department of Education

Timeline of sexual progress

The teenage years are a time of intense change, and lots of research shows that when "becoming sexual" starts to happen, it tends to follow a timeline, or a progression of intimate behaviors. You don't need to rush through this timeline or even follow the order, but it can be helpful to know how it works for some people.

Early on, your sex life might just be enjoying being horny when you're by yourself. If it's a date or a relationship, you might hold hands or kiss. A bit later, according to the research, young to mid-teens might start to engage in activities such as masturbation, which is where you touch your own genitals for sexual stimulation. Teens might watch online porn by themselves or start sexting. These behaviors might happen before any sort of physical contact with another person, but they are all types of sex and sexual behavior.

BEING HORNY

HOLDING HANDS

KISSING

TALKING ABOUT SEX

MASTURBATION

ONLINE CHAT

PICS

PORN

TALKING ABOUT SEX

DEEP KISSING

SEXUAL TOUCHING

TALKING ABOUT SEX

ORAL SEX

PENETRATIVE SEX

SEXUAL INTERCOURSE

TALKING ABOUT SEX

Deep kissing might also happen around this time, and a bit later, what we call **sexual touching**—touching and being touched on parts of the body that increase the body's sexual sensations. Things like oral sex usually happen toward the end of this sexual timeline. You might also decide to have sexual intercourse, or penetrative sex.

Any of the behaviors that involve you and another person—even if you're online and not in physical contact—automatically involve consent. It's important that *you* feel enthusiastic and positive about them, and that your partner does, too.

There have been people I know who have just gone with penetrative sex straightaway and then gone backward through the timeline—to kissing and hand-holding, and that's where they're at now. This was before we got a little talk about healthy relationships and stuff. *Noodles, 15*

More mythbusting

Here are some fun facts:

★ Plenty of teenagers finish high school before experiencing any of the above behaviors—and that is completely normal.

✳ Some people feel sexually turned on only by people of the same gender, or by more than one gender, or only by people of another gender. Some people don't feel sexual attraction at all.

✳ Sexual feelings and attractions can change over time.

★ Sex is designed by nature to be pleasurable, and it's therefore OK to expect pleasure.

Gender is a person's sense of being female, male, or something else. There's more to human beings than each person being either a "girl" or a "boy"—some people are somewhere in between, or neither. Some might have typical female chromosomes but identify as male and vice versa. It's all part of human diversity.

Figuring out what you like

So you've moved beyond crushes and kisses and you're ready to get more physically intimate with someone who is just as excited as you are. Yay! There could be cuddling and making out, or maybe you want to try touching each other elsewhere, like the breasts, bottom, thighs, back, penis, or vulva. You might have an *idea* about what's supposed to happen, but guess what? It's OK if you're really not sure. Navigate your own moments and allow them to evolve in a way that you're comfortable with!

During making-out sessions, one partner always followed the same pattern, and it was like a very solemn and serious ritual! My next partner was fun and chatty and it was much easier to say, "Hey, I love it when you do that" or "That doesn't feel so good." *Yumi*

Here's what we think are the most important things to remember:

★ Exploring your sexuality with another person, or on your own, should be fun. It can also be hilarious, awkward, silly, sexy, loud, and quiet. Whatever suits you is OK!

★ Nature designed sex to be pleasurable! So speak up if there's something you'd like more of or that you'd like to try. And if you're not into something, say so. Your partner would much rather you stop doing something you don't like than continue because you're too shy to say anything!

★ It is nice to be asked what you want, and to ask what someone else wants. That's also really helpful if you're new to this!

★ Try to tap into your own body and feelings, rather than "performing" for the other person. It's important to remember that often what we think we're supposed to do and like is influenced by TV, movies, and porn—which is usually *way off* from what people's actual needs, wants, and preferences are (see page 141).

★ Nothing you do should hurt. If you're doing something that hurts—and you didn't specifically want it to—you should stop right away.

★ Take turns leading! You don't have to always be in charge or always follow their lead.

★ Be open to change. You might have liked something last week, but this week it feels less good, and that's OK—just say so. Likewise, your partner might change what they want. It's important to keep talking to each other about what feels good and what doesn't.

★ Safety is no joke. If you and your partner have decided to have intercourse, then pregnancy and/or sexually transmitted infections could become a reality. See A NOTE FROM THE DOCTOR (Melissa) on page 156 to find out more. Consent involves each person understanding these potential consequences and agreeing to take steps to protect themselves. If one person refuses to use protection at the other person's request, for example, you can withdraw your consent to have intercourse with them.

REMEMBER: CONSENT IS A TWO-WAY STREET! EVEN IF YOU'VE BEEN WITH THE SAME PERSON FOR FIFTY YEARS, YOU STILL NEED TO MAKE SURE THAT YOU'RE BOTH ON THE SAME PAGE WHEN YOU'RE INTIMATE.

The "ruining the moment" myth

> When we asked young people, "How do you ask for what you want in a relationship?" the one thing that came out with absolute consensus was that *you must never ask for what you want sexually* because that "destroys romance" or "ruins the moment." I really want to emphasize that talking about what you want sexually does **not** destroy romance. It's the opposite! *Professor Alan McKee*

We cannot emphasize this enough: asking if everything is OK does not ruin the moment. Checking in does not ruin the moment. Asking to pause so that you or your partner can use contraception does not ruin the moment. Asking for what you want does not ruin the moment! And saying "Can we slow down?" just *slows things down*. All of these things are part of clear communication and consent. And here's a secret: all of these things will actually make the moment *so* much more enjoyable for both of you!

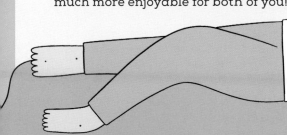

It is especially important to ask if you're doing these things together for the first time.

Consent is always important, even if you've been with someone for a long time. When you know someone well or have been intimate with them a few times, you might start to learn their specific behaviors or nonverbal ways of expressing consent, like looking at you in a particular way when they want to kiss you. But if you're in doubt, check in!

Navigate your own moments and allow them to evolve in a way that you're comfortable with.

> Thinking that you have to ask for consent can seem like a mood killer. But you always have to ask permission to do certain things. "Implied consent" isn't enough—you definitely need to learn the words. *Jackson,* **22**

In the real world, intimacy is not a silent, choreographed performance. People frequently check in with each other, give feedback, and make jokes. It's OK to say, for example, "Ouch, you're leaning on my hair!" The moment is *not* ruined. You're just communicating.

THINGS THAT DON'T RUIN THE MOMENT

THINGS THAT DO RUIN THE MOMENT

Is this OK?

Should we clip our toenails?

Does this feel good?

Should we keep going?

Do you want to hear me fart?

My mom wants me to clean my room and I can't be bothered.

I really like that!

Can we go slow?

Dairy gives me diarrhea.

I might have a bad cold right now.

Just checking in. You OK?

Let me know if you want a pause.

I think that seagull over there has lice.

151

Are you sure you can't ruin the moment?

Oh my god, *yes*, we're sure. (It's actually really hard to ruin the moment if you both want to be there.) And even if the moment does go off the rails a bit, you can always make it back to that moment if that's what everyone wants.

For women, it is sometimes so hard to say no because we are trained in a gendered world, from a young age, to say yes and smile when we do it.
Professor Catharine Lumby

Personally, it would be very funny to me if someone said, "I think that seagull over there has lice" and I would love to belly laugh with my partner and then get back to whatever it was we were doing. *Yumi*

THE RIGHT TO EXPECT PLEASURE

> You realize that the most important thing is your own happiness. Pleasure and happiness are intertwined. If you're truly happy and you're truly being respectful of yourself, you'll feel true pleasure. *Mel Ree*

Being physically intimate with someone, and having sex, is *much* more fun if you're both into it. That's the good news. If it feels great, you're doing it right.

The bad news is that every expert we interviewed for this book agreed that girls in heterosexual partnerships aren't expecting enough pleasure from sex. That's such a shame, because sex should be fun and pleasurable for *everyone*! If boys get intimate expecting to feel pleasure, so should girls!

This fact also rings true when I speak with teens as a doctor, or when I read their anonymous questions to the teen magazine health column, Dolly Doctor. Girls certainly feel horny as much as boys but find that when it comes to having sex with a boy, it's his pleasure that takes priority. *Dr. Melissa*

This can, in our opinion, sometimes make consent confusing. Not just in hetero relationships, either—in any kind of relationship! When there's an ongoing pleasure imbalance that favors one person over the other, it's perfectly reasonable to question whether it's something you want to keep doing. On the other hand, you like giving your partner pleasure! That's why communication about what each person likes, doesn't like, or wants more of is so important. Understanding that a girl's pleasure is as meaningful, achievable, and worthy as a boy's will help you draw boundaries around things that might not feel good for either of you.

If anyone is feeling discomfort, disgust, or pain, that is 100 percent not supposed to be part of the package, and you should stop. Maybe you're not ready for it. Maybe it's not your thing. Or maybe you're not doing it right!

There is no sexual act so important that anyone should have to endure unwanted pain for it to continue.

Our advice is to take your time and trust that you know your body best. Everyone, whatever their gender or sexuality, deserves to experience pleasure in a joyful atmosphere of mutual consent.

I remember making a pact with myself—I decided I'm going to honor my body more. I'm not going to go through with sex because I feel obligated. It's like—your memories are how you decorate the interior of your head. And I want it to be nice in there! *Nick Pezza*

As we get older and start to explore our bodies in a sexual way, one of the most important things is knowing what feels good for you. And that's what makes masturbation so important. So learning to understand what feels good for you is a really important part of learning what feels wrong. *Professor Catharine Lumby*

A NOTE FROM THE DOCTOR (MELISSA)

Have you seen the movie *Clueless*? There's a scene where the main character, Cher, explains why she hasn't had sex with anyone: "You see how picky I am about my shoes, and they only go on my feet!" In this moment, Cher's fifteen-year-old self exudes a gentle confidence about her boundaries and respect for her bodily autonomy.

Being sexually healthy is about more than just being physically well—it's about our mental health, too. It comes from self-respect and being able to enjoy consensual, intimate experiences with other people on mutual terms. These steps toward sexual health start way before you're actually having sex.

Sexual health is also about avoiding some of the negative physical consequences of sex, such as unplanned pregnancies or infections. That might be a long way off for you, or not. Whatever your gender or sexuality, you have the right to confidential advice from a doctor. Doctors can give you information, prescribe contraception, offer testing and treatment for STIs (sexually transmitted infections), or discuss pregnancy.

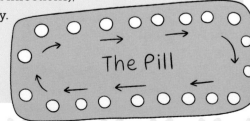

The Pill

Avoiding pregnancy and STIs

Teens usually learn about condoms from health class at school, and for good reason. They are not only a good contraceptive (something that can prevent pregnancy), they're also the best protection against STIs. You can buy them in different places (supermarkets, convenience stores, pharmacies, vending machines, gas stations) and don't need proof of age or ID.

Sometimes you might want—and need— some more specific advice about your sexual health. For example, preventing pregnancy is not an issue if your partners are the same sex as you. Or you might be unsure about STIs because what you learned in school focused mainly on heterosexual couples. Or you might simply want to know more about sexual health than what you've learned in health class.

If avoiding pregnancy is relevant for you, it's definitely worth visiting your doctor to look at your options. There are prescription contraceptives that are close to 100 percent effective for preventing pregnancy (condoms are around 90 percent effective). Using a prescription contraceptive doesn't mean ditching condoms. It's fine—and often sensible—to use both.

LUBE

Getting an STI test is another way to look after your sexual health. Most teens with an STI won't have symptoms. Getting tested means you get treated early if you do have an STI, and it stops you from passing it on to someone else. For most teens, it's a simple urine test. Your doctor can give you advice about whether additional tests are appropriate.

Confidentiality

So how do you actually get to a doctor, and how do you know you can trust them to keep it confidential?

Most teens rely on a parent or caregiver to make a doctor's appointment, take them there, and help get prescriptions filled. As you grow up—and start doing more adult things, like having sex—you might want to start seeing a doctor on your own. Some teens are comfortable talking to a parent about sex. And— note to parents!—research shows that when parents talk to their teens about sexual health, the teens are more likely to have safer sex at a time when they're ready for it.

> I don't know how to make my own doctor's appointment. I tend to have it done for me.
> *Tans, 15*

What's important to know is that you have the right to see a doctor whether your parents are involved or not. You can see the family doctor who you've known forever, or you might want to find your own doctor or a health center. Your parent might help you do that! Or a friend or older sibling might recommend someone they see. Be mindful of how the visit is being paid for, though—depending on your insurance, your family may see a bill or statement.

By law, doctors must keep information that their patients share with them confidential. The main exceptions are if:

1 A parent requests their child's health information.

2 You tell the doctor that they can talk to a specific other person about it.

3 The doctor thinks you are at risk of seriously harming yourself or someone else.

4 The doctor believes you are being seriously harmed or abused. By law, doctors must report this in order to keep you safe from further harm.

MORE ON p. 163

There have been situations where I have seen the doctor and I say, "I don't want you to release that to my parents."
Corey, 17

You are totally allowed to go to the doctor on your own, without a parent or guardian. If you plan on going alone, you can contact the doctor's office beforehand to see if they need any information from your parents or guardians.

Law and the age of consent

You might have heard the expression **age of consent**. It refers to the age at which you can legally consent to having sex.

These laws were made to protect children because throughout history, in some cases, girls could legally be married off at very young ages. That meant their older husbands could legally have sex with them—and the idea of the girl being asked to consent was really *not* a thing. Teens were also abused or coerced into sex by older people, usually without any legal consequences.

Today, it's much better! The law sets a minimum age that you can *legally* consent to sex, which depends on the state you live in, as well as other circumstances. And those laws are still very much about protecting you—it's not you, but the person who's having sex with you, who is breaking the law.

It might feel like you are a sexual and grown-up person, in full control of your desires and your body. But there can be a big power difference between you and someone who is even a few years older than you. This power imbalance can lead to manipulation and exploitation—sometimes without you even realizing it.

MORE ON p. 96

Because the law understands that power imbalances exist, there is an extra part to the age-of-consent laws when it comes to certain people who play supervisory roles in a teen's life. Different state laws regulate whether or when people in a position of power, such as teachers, sports coaches, foster caregivers, or religious instructors, can have sex with people under their supervision or care.

In law-speak, what is sex?

The law defines *sex* as more than just penis-in-vagina sex. Specifics vary across the country, but sex *can* include putting anything inside ("penetrating") the vagina or anus and any kind of oral sex.

Does that mean everyone under the age of consent is breaking the law when they have sex?

No. Not everyone under the age of consent is breaking the law if they have sex. Many state laws recognize that teens of a *similar age* can have sex (using the legal definition above) with mutual consent. This may mean that if one or both people are under the age of consent but of a similar age (less than two or three years apart, depending on the state), and both consent to sex, it isn't considered a crime.

Each state has its own *absolute lowest age limit* that says no matter how close in age two people are, they are still too young to consent to sex.

You might hear that lots of teens are having sex. Maybe it seems like a lot of the teens you know are. But statistically speaking, most high schoolers have *not* had sexual intercourse.

GIVING CONSENT ALWAYS MATTERS, REGARDLESS OF AGE.

AS ALWAYS, IF THERE HAS NOT BEEN CONSENT IN A SEXUAL ENCOUNTER, IT'S A CRIME NO MATTER HOW YOUNG OR OLD A PERSON IS.

Don't freak out

MORE ON p. 96

Age-of-consent laws are there to look out for teens and children. An older person who knowingly tries to engage you in intimate, sexual acts when you are below the age of consent is—frankly—a creep.

But if you're sexually active with someone close to your age and it's consensual (both parties consent, every time), then you're very unlikely to get in trouble. This is especially true if you and your partner can take all the necessary steps to look after birth control and your sexual health.

Health professionals do not have to report giving advice about sex and sexual health to a teen to the police. If the health professional believes the teen is being abused, then they need to discuss this with a child protection agency, which is designed to look out for the teen and keep them safe. *Dr. Melissa*

Contraceptive laws for minors vary from state to state in the US. Here are some scenarios Dr. Melissa has seen over the years in Australia:

ALICE AND MATEO

Alice and Mateo are fifteen years old, have been dating for a few months, and want to start having sexual intercourse. Alice comes to see me to talk about contraception. We talk about her health, but also about this situation—she fully consents to a sexual relationship with Mateo, and he even offered to come with her to this appointment.

As we talk, it is clear that she understands the information we discuss about contraception, sex, and, importantly, consent. We talk a bit about her family and whether she has spoken to a parent about her relationship. I believe she is *not* being abused by Mateo (or anyone else), and so I do not have to report this to anyone. Alice's discussion with me is confidential, and she is mature enough to consent to me prescribing contraception.

CHRISSIE AND STEVE

Chrissie is fifteen years old and has had sex once before with someone her age. She met Steve online and they have hooked up a few times, including to have sex. Steve is twenty-five and tells Chrissie she looks eighteen and "seems older" and that he's really into her. He's also told Chrissie to "go get the implant" (a long-term contraceptive device implanted into the arm by a doctor) because he doesn't want babies.

In this situation, even though Chrissie is sexually experienced and mature for a fifteen-year-old, the age difference is sufficient for me to feel that the relationship is abusive and there is a big power difference between Chrissie and Steve. On top of that, he is pressuring her about the contraceptive implant. In this situation I will explain my concerns to Chrissie and tell her that I need to make a report to a child protection agency who will want to look into this situation and keep her safe.

CONSENT IN RELATIONSHIPS

Beginning a relationship with someone can be the most amazing, terrifying, and exciting feeling. Amazing to know someone likes you back. Terrifying because you don't want to lose them. And exciting because it's something new you can explore together!

Your conversations around consent—on everything from which movie to see to what exactly you want to do sexually—will continue throughout your relationship, even after you've been together for a while.

Have you noticed how your moods change depending on a bunch of factors—being hungry, your period, getting in trouble, a bad night's sleep? In the same way, what feels good and right sexually can change depending on the day. Being with the same person doesn't change that. What you want to happen to your body can be different *every single time*. Just because you wanted something one day doesn't mean you want it again!

This applies to your partner, too—the one you're with now or someone in the future. Their needs and preferences won't be the same each time. You need to check in again (and again).

All the golden rules of consent still apply in a relationship. You can change your mind at any time if you want to. You can stop having any kind of sex once you've started, or choose not to do a particular thing again, in person or online.

Ignoring your nonconsent is wrong. Nonconsensual behavior in a relationship can be things like persistent begging for sex, sulking if sex is refused, or threatening to self-harm, to end the relationship, or to seek sex elsewhere. **THIS IS NOT COOL.** It's called **sexual coercion**. Hopefully, by being aware of consent and the magic that open communication can create, you can recognize this if it happens—and call it out. And if something feels off, or you're being pressured to do something you don't like, you should talk to someone in your safety network about that. It never hurts to say, "Does this sound right to you?" or "Can you help me figure out what I should do next?"

Honesty and vulnerability

It can feel embarrassing talking about what you want when you're being physically intimate with someone. What we see modeled for us on TV or in porn isn't very verbal—people just "magically" seem to know, or they guess. Well, in the real world, that doesn't work.

When we talk about being vulnerable, we are talking about exposing those feelings of embarrassment or shyness. Not everyone feels vulnerable in that way, but it can be tough for others.

Being honest and vulnerable with your partner is the best way to eventually have an amazing, joyful, and super-fun time. Getting there takes practice. Don't be afraid to fail. There are ways to start the conversation that make it easier:

★ "I'm feeling a bit scared, but I want to tell you what I'm into, and I really want you to tell me what you're into!"

★ "Do you want to try some things? Only things that you *really* want to do."

★ "There's something I've always wanted to do with you . . ."

168

One of my good friends had a partner who, whenever they started getting intimate, would do something that put her off. (I asked her to tell me what it was, but she refused!) She was too scared to say anything to him about it because she didn't want to hurt his feelings! It was so bad she avoided all sex with him just because she didn't want him to do that one thing. *Anonymous*

I pretended I'd had sex before! I wanted to seem experienced, so I pretended! I think the message I learned from that was that it's OK to be vulnerable and it's OK to be honest. If I had been honest, we would've taken it slowly and both of us would've enjoyed it more. *Professor Catharine Lumby*

I think it's hot. It's really sexy to say, "Can I take this off?" Treating your partner or even your friends as precious, and someone you really respect and you want to take care with—I think that is hot and loving. *Sally Rugg*

Safe words

A safe word is a word that you've agreed to use if one of you wants to quickly stop whatever action it is you're doing. It's usually chosen as a word you'd never accidentally say during sex or physical intimacy.

> Safe words are commonly talked about at our school. We talk about how you don't even have to be having a sexual relationship to have a safe word. My good friends have just started dating and they love banter, but if the teasing gets to the point where they feel uncomfortable, one of them will say "Lamborghini!" *Miranda, 16*

It's good to decide what using the safe word means. Usually it means "stop all action immediately." But you might want to have a chat about it before you get started. It could mean "pause." You could be bantering, doing role-play, or tickling, and it's a way to say, "I've stopped enjoying this."

Using the safe word doesn't mean disaster has struck. It means you've had a conversation about consent, you have agreed on a pathway to communicate something very clearly, and one of you has chosen to use it.

Safe words you can use include:

STINK BUG

ORANGE JUICE

GORGONZOLA

KENDRICK LAMAR

DOLLY PARTON

For nonverbal communicators, the "safe word" can be a gesture, wink, or hand symbol, or holding on to an object that you drop to say "stop." Again, you want to use something that you wouldn't commonly use during intimacy, like a peace sign, a firm tap on the shoulder, or a T for *time-out*.

I think Red Yellow Green should be 100 percent mainstream. Red is STOP; we need to END what we're doing; I'm at my limit. Yellow is the really important one. It means, let's keep doing what we're doing, but no more; I might be at my limit. I'm cool with where we are but no more. Green is HELL YEAH, everything is awesome! *Ally Garrett*

HOOKUPS: RESPECT IN THE MOMENT

Hooking up can mean anything from making out, kissing and cuddling, sexual touching, or oral sex to having penetrative sex—usually outside of a serious relationship. These things can *lead* to a relationship, but at the time of the hookup, monogamy and "love" are not assumed.

Not everyone goes into a hookup with the same intention. Sometimes people just want to have fun, be close, or explore a connection or spark with someone. We're not here to judge, but it's important to ensure there is respect established between you and the other person, and that you are both enthusiastically consenting partners.

Respect in the moment is about humanizing your partner (not just using their body for your own pleasure), respecting them and their boundaries, and being honest. It prioritizes consent, because you may not know each other well, and you can't assume anything about the other's boundaries.

Respecting your hookup partner in the moments you hook up is important because, for however long your interaction lasts, your attention is on them and theirs on you. It also means understanding that a lot, and sometimes all, of what occurs between you two is private unless you've both agreed otherwise.

Often with gay hookups, you have that consent conversation ahead of time, because it's less of a given as to what goes where and who's doing what. You communicate *really* explicitly because you want to make sure you're compatible before you make the effort. *Billy J. Russell*

It also means not lying. Unfortunately, sometimes people (of any sex or gender) think they have to lie to get a hookup and pretend that they're looking for a relationship when they're not. It's so unnecessary! Most people can stand hearing the truth and would prefer it.

He was (or seemed like) the sweetest guy. Took me on cute dates, really cuddly, didn't sleep with me until the fifth date because he "really liked me" and "thought it could be serious." Then I literally *never* heard from him again. He dropped off the face of the earth. What confused me was that I would have happily hooked up with him on a casual basis—he set me up to really like him. *Abby Edwards*

CONSENT *Challenges*

Double dates and setups

Sometimes people try to set you up on a date because they *really* think you'll like a particular person. Sometimes it's just because you're both single. And sometimes they just want company on a double date while they spend time with their boyfriend or girlfriend or partner.

Setups can be fun, but they are often thoughtlessly put together—the only criterion applied is that you're both single, with no consideration given to your personalities!

You might go on a *date* date, or you might just go to a party together. Either way, sometimes it can feel like there's a lot of pressure to hook up, which can really work against consent. But if you're in a setup and you don't like it, you absolutely *don't* have to do anything you don't want to do.

Sitting through a "date" with someone you don't like may seem like an eternity of discomfort and boredom, but what's *worse* is pretending to like someone and making out with them just to be polite.

The best thing to do is communicate that you're not into it and look for something else to do. You could even go for "frank and charming" and say something like, "Hey, you seem cool, but I'm not really feeling the spark. Want to do something else instead?"

I got there and the guy was physically not my type. The way he talked was just not my type. I definitely felt pressure. While they're doing their thing, what are we meant to do? I felt way too uncomfortable, so I never actually did anything. *Lana, 17*

I once got set up with my friend's boyfriend's friend who went to another school, and he turned out to be great—we really liked each other! It was such a relief. We had lots to talk about and ended up swapping numbers that day. We dated for eight months afterward. *Marisa, 36*

CONSENT
Challenges

Under pressure: sex

> Maybe you want to believe that you're ready for it, even though you're not. There are expectations, too, like, "Maybe I'm supposed to have had sex by now?" The pressure is me worrying that I'm too old to say no. Even if I want to. *Miranda, 16*

Sometimes we're dying to check off new experiences. Other times we feel like we have to catch up to what our friends are doing or we'll be left behind. And sometimes we can't even tell *where* the pressure is coming from—it just feels like a lot.

If you feel like there's pressure to do something, it's a good idea to take a minute to check in with your feelings. You might find that you genuinely feel ready to do it, regardless of everyone else; or you might realize that you really, really don't. Remember that this whole thing (*points to your body*) is yours. You're the boss of it. You do things when you're ready.

MORE ON p. 72

> A lot of people think that peer pressure is a group thing—but if someone is trying to obtain something sexually from you, it doesn't actually take a whole group of people to push you into that zone. You can be persuaded by one individual whispering in your ear. *Luke, 17*

With a partner

When you're with someone you really like, but you don't feel ready for sexual stuff, it can be hard to resist feelings of pressure. But if one person wants to do more, and the other wants to do less—you should always choose the *less* option.

The same is true whether you're the one who wants to do less or the one who wants to do more.

It's OK to do less. The feeling that it's urgent, that you need to do it all, or that you'll be dumped if you don't agree to do something—that's common. But life is long. There will be plenty more chances to do everything you want to do in your future. And remember, anyone who would dump you for not consenting to something you don't want to do isn't cool. (They're actually gross!)

Even if the other person doesn't agree with your boundaries (for example, "You can touch me over my clothes, but not under"), that doesn't matter. The other person might get confused or annoyed, and you may even wonder, *If these two options are so close, is it really worth starting an argument about what I've said yes to and what I'm saying no to?*

The answer is—yes! Just because two acts are similar doesn't mean you're OK with both. And just because you want to withhold consent for one particular activity, that does not mean *all* activity has to stop.

As the boss of your body, you get to draw boundaries around what you will and won't do. Your partner should accept your call on what you want for your body, and vice versa.

YES

NO

Because you know each other, you can ask the questions that are harder to ask when you first start seeing each other. You're also much better at reading their body language and getting the cues. *Billy*

CONSENT
Challenges

Sexting

Sending nude pics online and texting sexual banter (aka sexting) is a way for people in committed or casual relationships to deepen their connection and explore sex when they're not together. Like everything about human sexuality, it's not for everyone, and that's OK. In fact, research reflects this: some young people who engage in sexting are confident and feel good about it, while others feel the opposite.

In an ideal world, texting nudes should be pretty cool—you can't get pregnant, you can't catch any diseases, you can log out or switch off if it's getting to be too much, and you don't even have to smell nice when you're doing it.

But things can go wrong, and it's all to do with consent. If two people want to share intimate stuff online with each other, consent still has to apply—just as if they were sharing intimate stuff in person.

MORE ON p. 96

The world of sexting can highlight the way gender and power issues operate as well. Plenty of research among teens has shown that girls often feel pressured to send nude pics to boys, that they are more likely to get "reputations" if they do, and that boys feel pressured to share a girl's nudes with other boys without getting the girl's consent. Like any behavior that is disrespectful or discriminatory, let's call it out!

I know a lot of people have expectations with girls—I've come across a few guys who have been surprised when I've said, "No, I don't want to send anything" (and by that I mean nudes), and they've just been surprised because "every girl does it"—but not every girl does. *Chloe, 17*

The internet is permanent, and because you can't control where stuff goes once it's out there, it's probably best not to send pics. But that can be like saying, "It's best you don't fart." Yeah, it's best we don't fart, but smell the air—someone around here is farting!

Deciding to send nudes should be like deciding to engage in other intimate behaviors. Talk about it first. If you're someone with a penis, it's polite to ask *before* you send someone a dick pic. (Surprise dick pics are often bad surprises.) And no matter what your body looks like in the pic, make clear what you are and are not consenting to by sharing the picture. You could say something like, "I don't want you to share this with anyone. It's just between us. And please delete it once you've seen it."

My bf and I send photos to each other all the time, but I always crop my face out so I can't be identified. Those photos could go to my *mother* and she wouldn't be 100 percent sure it was me. *Lee, 17*

There's a girl in our grade who sent a nude picture of herself to her maybe-partner at the time. And it got shared around. A police officer had to step in and take care of it. *Drishti, 14*

Usually how it goes is someone asks for a photo. The person who's sending the pic usually sets some kind of terms, like, no sharing, no screenshots. But are those terms followed? Not always. *Luke, 17*

GOLDEN RULES

1. Don't share pictures or videos of someone without their consent—even if they willingly sent it to you.

2. If it's a picture or video showing someone under eighteen years old without their clothes on—even if it's you—you're wading into territory that could be illegal.

3. Don't send pics to someone you don't know in real life.

4. If someone threatens you about pictures, tell an adult you can trust or call one of the services we've listed on page 200. Even if you've already sent a pic, you won't get in trouble if you're asking for help. It's going to be OK.

I worked in youth law, and many young people contacted us to say they'd sent a nude pic or video and the person then threatened to spread it unless they sent more. It was terrifying for the kids. My advice: do *not* send any more nudes to that person, and get help. You're not the first person this has happened to, and there are organizations set up to help. *Marty James*

SEXUAL OR NUDE PICTURES OF PEOPLE UNDER 18 ARE CONSIDERED CHILD PORNOGRAPHY, WHICH IS **ILLEGAL**. GENERALLY, IT IS ILLEGAL TO ASK FOR IT, TO SEND IT, AND TO SHARE IT. THERE ARE PROTECTIONS FOR PEOPLE WHO REPORT IT TO THE POLICE.

THE LAW

There are many state laws to protect you when sexting. They become stricter if you are under eighteen. The laws vary from state to state and country to country and are being updated regularly, so check in with what the law says in your territory before sending or receiving nude pics.

CONSENT
Challenges

When you're drinking

When it comes to alcohol, it's less of a consent "challenge" and more of a minefield!

You may not be drinking alcohol right now—the legal drinking age in America is twenty-one—but it's important to know that it changes the way people think and feel, and therefore influences how people act. The more alcohol someone drinks, the bigger the change. With one or two standard drinks, they might be more social and outgoing. With more, they may get pretty drunk: slurring their speech, falling down, and becoming aggressive. And if they keep drinking, they might black out, vomit, and not remember what they did or said the next day.

Of course, if you're young or new to drinking alcohol, it might take a lot less than a few standard drinks to get you drunk—and it's unpredictable. Even one drink can have a big impact.

Here's what you need to know about alcohol and consent: a person can't consent at all if they are drunk. Even if they appear to be enthusiastically consenting, being wasted means they are incapable of giving consent. The law is pretty strict about this, no matter how old you are. The same goes when you're high: you can't legally consent.

However, there is a weird gray zone if you're a little bit drunk. The law doesn't explicitly state how sober a person needs to be to make an informed decision to consent. In sexual assault cases in which alcohol or other drugs have been present, it's up to a judge to decide if a complainant was too drunk to consent.

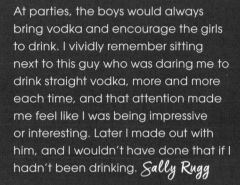

At parties, the boys would always bring vodka and encourage the girls to drink. I vividly remember sitting next to this guy who was daring me to drink straight vodka, more and more each time, and that attention made me feel like I was being impressive or interesting. Later I made out with him, and I wouldn't have done that if I hadn't been drinking. *Sally Rugg*

DRINKING: PARENTS AND THE LAW

The law is pretty clear around parents giving their kids alcohol: adults usually are allowed to give their own kids a little bit of alcohol at home, under supervision. It varies from state to state, but nowhere is "free-range drinking" by underage kids legal.

WHAT IS A STANDARD DRINK?

A "standard drink" depends on the strength of the alcohol and relates to roughly how much an adult body can process in an hour. But confusingly, one drink—say, a can of beer or a glass of wine—is often more than a standard drink.

To give you an idea:

1.5 ounces distilled alcohol = 1 standard drink

5 ounces wine = 1 standard drink

12 ounces beer = 1 standard drink

What do teens say?

In research that looked at the reasons why teens (of all genders) had sex when they didn't want to, almost 50 percent said it was because they were too drunk or high. They were basically saying they didn't want to have sex and they couldn't consent.

If you plan on drinking, you need to be extra careful about setting your boundaries and keeping yourself safe— as well as treating other people with respect.

If you choose to drink—even as an adult—there are some things you can do to keep yourself safe:

1. **Don't rush.** The effects of alcohol can really sneak up on you. It's easy to drink too fast (especially sugary, fizzy drinks) and then be *really* drunk a short time later. Go slow. Eat something, alternate alcoholic drinks with water or other nonalcoholic drinks, and don't drink on an empty stomach.

2. **Own it.** Be realistic and honest about how much you are hoping/planning to drink and let your friends know whether they may need to take care of you.

3. **Pay attention to how you feel.** Don't just drink automatically. Are you drinking because you're thirsty? Stop and have some water. Are you drinking because you're nervous? Stop and find a friend who will make you feel better. Or consider whether you really want to be there at all.

4. **Stay close to friends.** Look after your friends, and ask them to look after you. Make an agreement that if you see each other acting out of character or in a weird situation, you'll step in and help. Talk about sharing locations on your phones. If there's a nondrinker in your group, that's the best—especially if you can trust them to look out for you.

5. **Get out.** Have a definite exit plan, with backup, and make the plan clear before you start drinking. How are you getting home? Do you all agree on this? Does a trusted adult know? And what if your ride cancels or you can't find one of your group when it's time to go? Talk it through; assess your options. If one of your friends has a habit of disappearing, call them on it and talk it through.

6 Panic button. **Part of growing up means we want to rely less on our parents—we want to exert our independence. But that doesn't mean you should remain in a dangerous situation out of pride! Hitting the panic button can mean calling a parent and asking them to come and get you, spending money you hadn't budgeted for on a ride, or calling the police or an ambulance.**

I know this is not realistic advice to give teenagers, and yet it's good advice: alcohol is a dangerous, addictive drug. For this reason, I choose not to drink—ever. *Yumi*

The tricky thing about drinking

Drinking alcohol commonly leads to poor judgment around many things—including consent. It might mean you end up in dangerous situations, taking risks and ignoring your gut instincts. It can also mean more impulsive behavior— you might be more excited and less likely to consider the consequences of your actions.

It's worth taking alcohol seriously—if you care about your own consent and your friends' consent, then you need to take measures to stay safe when drinking.

Alcohol is involved in over one-third of the sexual assault cases that I see involving teenagers. In these cases, the teenager has not been able to give consent. *Dr. Tania May*

TO BE VERY CLEAR: DRINKING OR BEING AROUND PEOPLE WHO HAVE BEEN DRINKING ALCOHOL DOES NOT MAKE IT YOUR FAULT IF YOU'RE ASSAULTED. BUT IF YOU'RE DRINKING, YOU ARE LESS ABLE TO DETECT— AND AVOID—DANGEROUS SITUATIONS.

If someone is intoxicated to a concerning level, like if they can't hold their head up, I'll often ask their full name, their mother's maiden name, their home address. If they can't answer, that's when me and my friends know to call an ambulance, because it's better to be safe than sorry. *Kera, 18*

CALLING OUT THE ADULTS

We wrote this book to look at situations involving consent that you might encounter with *people your age* as you grow up.

We want to be very clear that adults who overstep boundaries, behave inappropriately, or harass, abuse, or assault children and teens must be called out and stopped. Fortunately there is now much more awareness, education, and legal backup to address and prevent such behavior compared to when we were kids. But we're also aware that it's still far too common.

Some teens we spoke to talked about "creepy teachers" who made them feel uncomfortable. It might have been the way they looked at them, or they got a bit flirty. Others have had that icky feeling with a coach or a boss.

To understand how to stick up for yourself in such situations, it's helpful to know how solid the rules are: no abuse, no "romance," no threats. The law backs you up. This applies to *anyone* in a position of authority over you.

If an adult is making you feel uncomfortable or frightened, you don't need to keep it a secret. Write down an account of what has happened, and then tell your parents or guardians. Tell someone in your safety network. Tell another adult you trust. Take it up the chain of command (in other words, tell their boss, such as the principal).

Most child abusers are someone the child knows—often a family member. It might be someone you love or thought you could trust. This means that feelings of confusion and fear can be profound. There is no circumstance where child or teen sexual abuse is OK—not in any culture, religion, or family setup.

No matter how terrifying it seems, there is always an adult—many, in fact—who can and will help. It could be a trusted teacher who helps you take that first step in seeking help. It might be a parent, youth worker, doctor, or counselor.

We've compiled a list of resources and services that are especially for kids and teens who have been abused by adults (page 203). We sincerely hope you never have to use it. But it's here if you do.

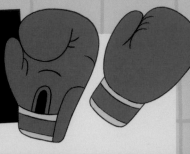

FIGHT, FLIGHT, FREEZE, APPEASE

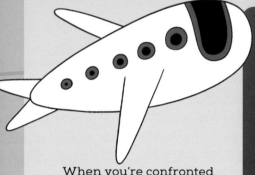

When I was in seventh grade, I was in a car accident with my family on the way to school. A guy who was asleep at the wheel ran into us. It wasn't a major accident but he was *very* angry, and I think my fight or flight reflex kicked in because I started yelling at him—it was a lot of adrenaline. *Chloe, 17*

When you're confronted by a threat, your body's instinctive physical reactions kick into gear. So, for instance, if confronted by an angry parent, your instinct might be to shout back and "fight." But if confronted by a lion, your instinct might be to run—"flight." In both fight and flight, your body experiences a surge of adrenaline that helps you to optimize your strength, speed, and wits.

These are commonly recognized reactions. But there are two more:

FREEZE and

APPEASE.

Freeze is the most common bodily response to sexual assault and sexual violence—and lots of different trauma. Freeze is the first response. That's why checking in is so important. When your body is in freeze mode, it's just trying to survive. *Saxon Mullins*

When I was out with my mom, I was approached by a man. My mom was somewhere else ordering food, and I just froze because I didn't know what I could say. I was kind of shocked at myself and I thought I could have handled it better. I could have done so many things rather than just freeze in that moment. *Yosh, 14*

When someone "freezes" in a dangerous situation, their body is trying to protect them. It is an evolutionary survival tactic, similar to when an animal plays dead. People who have frozen in response to danger can feel really confused about their reaction—*Why didn't I do something? Why didn't I shout? Or fight?* Even those who are trained in combat or self-defense can have a freeze reaction when their body is threatened. This is another reason why it's so important to check in with your friends and partners when you're doing something new. If they're having a freeze reaction, they might not be able to tell you. Give them the time and space they need to process things and respond to you, and check in on them again soon after to make sure they're OK.

Appease is a word to describe trying to go along with or even being friendly toward the person who has threatened or assaulted you. This can mean trying to keep the peace for as long as is necessary until the situation feels less dangerous or it's safe to escape. In real terms it could mean hanging out or even going out for a drink with the person who assaulted you right after the incident.

What follows is often a negotiation in the survivor's head along the lines of, "If I just pretend to go along with him and be a good and entertaining girl, I can get away." Anyone who has a dog knows what appeasement looks like. The dog who feels threatened rolls over and submits to avoid a potentially more vicious attack. Women have been trained—some less successfully than others—to please other people and to avoid male anger and violence.

Professor Catharine Lumby

I tend to freeze up—you have to do a really, really fast calculation of whether the danger you're in is going to escalate or dissipate, depending on your next step. For instance, when I was a teenager, I was groped on the subway by a stranger. In my school uniform! Gross. In a moment I had to make a split-second assessment: Who else is on the train? If I say something, is someone going to back me up? *Sally Rugg*

WHEN THINGS DON'T FEEL RIGHT

We can't emphasize enough how important it is to listen to your gut and trust your instincts.

We have heard many stories about people going through with an intimate act because they were afraid of what would happen if they said no. They didn't want the action to continue but were afraid that it would be *worse* to say no, so they reluctantly allowed it to go on.

It's not just sex or intimacy. Your instincts could tell you not to get into a car with someone who seems a bit off. Or to back out of a situation that suddenly seems really stupid and unsafe. It might happen with someone online, too. Your intuition comes from within, no matter what the context. In these moments, it's critical that you listen to that instinct and get out.

It doesn't matter if you look dumb or like you've overreacted. So what if you did? Trust that your gut knows what it's doing and is trying to keep you safe.

This is a good spot to remind you that *safety is vital for true consent to occur.* Extreme examples of not being safe are easy to identify—for example, what if a stranger were holding you by the throat? But needing to feel safe also applies in situations where you suddenly feel like you're not in control and need to trust your gut, like:

- ★ You're suddenly separated from your friends and feel quite vulnerable.
- ✴ You don't want your parents to find out what you've been doing, and this person could tell them.
- ✴ You're alone with someone you don't know very well.
- ★ They're able-bodied and you're not.
- ★ They have something you need to feel safe, like your phone or money.

Sometimes the feeling of disempowerment, the inability to say no, is so subtle that you can convince yourself to go along with the situation. You want to stay safe. You don't want to cause trouble. But consent, in this case, has not been freely given.

My gut feeling said, "He's not sober." It was only a two-second interaction, but I got the vibe that he was not all there. I ended up getting in a car with him, and he drove like a psycho. An utter psycho. I could have died that day. I really could have. It was really bad.
Anouk, 18

> Most people's bodies often get to that unsafe feeling before their minds do. So that gut feeling of feeling a bit sick, pulse racing, that something is not right—sometimes it's hard to pinpoint what's wrong.
> *Dr. Ellie Freedman*

> That feeling has saved my life at least four times. I never let that feeling go on—I start going through all the scenarios that could happen, and how to take evasive action. I listen to that feeling 100 percent. It's there to help you. *Imogen Kelly*

Make sure you're safe

If you think you're in trouble, the first and most important thing you can do is get yourself to a safe place:

- ★ **Remove yourself from the situation—say you need to use the bathroom, or get a drink of water. If possible, lock yourself in a room and call someone trustworthy for help.**

- ✳ **Call out to someone nearby if the situation allows.**

- ★ **Pretend you're taking a phone call and move away.**

- If it's feasible, walk away completely.

- Call a parent, caregiver, or safe adult—even if you think they'll get mad. They might, but it's still better to be safe.

- If the situation is online, switch off the app, or your phone, or ignore the messages until you have the space to let the feeling that it isn't right settle, and you can think or talk it through with someone.

- If you aren't sure where to go, call or go directly to the police or a trusted resource that's safe for you.

Feeling unsafe can also make us feel isolated. When things don't feel right, whether it happens once or repeatedly, it's really important to know that support is out there. *You can feel safe again.* There are numbers in the back of this book that you can call if you need help deciding who to talk to. For more information about where to find support, go to SAFETY RESOURCES, page 199, and IF YOU NEED HELP, page 201.

> At those parties, I would excuse myself to go to the bathroom, saying, "I'll be back in a minute, get me a drink!" And I'd leave the house and call my parents. Or I'd just get myself out of there, walk myself home. I wouldn't stick around in a situation like that at all—I'd tell people around me or secure another ride.
> *Imogen Kelly*

One of the toughest parts of my job is seeing a young person who feels unsafe because of something that's happened. One of the best parts of my job is when I can almost feel, with them, the moment that feeling goes away, when they've found safety. *Dr. Melissa*

Safety resources

Knowing your rights and how to stick up for them is the best way to stay safe. But even that won't make you bulletproof.

All those hotlines are absolute gold. Get on the phone and tell those people because they're trained, and they're incredible, and they give the best advice. *Imogen Kelly*

Contacts

A
Amal
B
Blake
C
chen
connie
D
Dad

IN CASE OF EMERGENCY

• Jenny •

Emergency Contacts...
• mom
• Dad
• Georgia

Now is a good time to add the phone numbers (or apps) of key people and resources to your phone. If you do urgently need help, having those numbers ready will make you one little step closer to safety. Get them now, and hopefully you won't need them.

MORE ON p. 204

* **Emergency services**

* **Childhelp National Child Abuse Hotline**

* **The people in your safety network**

* **Taxi/rideshare app**

* **Crisis counselor**

* **Sexual assault hotline**

* **Domestic violence hotline**

There are also apps that will let someone know if you're in distress. Some apps will contact a family member; others will go straight to the police. Discuss with your closest caregivers or friends which technology suits your situation. You're going to need to tell them if they're the person who gets the alert.

There is no magic potion (or book) that can keep you safe at all times. What you can be is *informed*. What you can do is your best.

IF YOU NEED HELP

We sincerely, truly hope that your boundaries are never crossed. But the world is a big place, and sometimes bad or hurtful things can happen. If you get hurt or feel your boundaries have been crossed, we have some suggestions for what to do next.

Ask for help

You deserve to be safe and to be loved, so you should not hesitate to ask someone for help. That person could be a parent, older sibling or family member, or someone else in your safety network. It could be a friend or your doctor. It could be the police.

If, for whatever reason, you feel your complaint has not been taken seriously, take it up the chain. Talk to someone else—maybe someone in a position of authority at your school. Make yourself heard. Don't be discouraged if some jerk is disrespecting you; just keep asking other people until someone helps you. We can't emphasize enough how important it is to turn to a trusted adult.

Assault is not your fault

Most of us move through the world hoping to avoid pain, injury, humiliation, and conflict. If you have been the victim of sexual assault, you might wonder whether you took the right "precautions" to avoid it. You may ruminate on how to prevent it from happening again. But no matter what happened, what you were wearing, where you were, whether you were drinking or asleep—if something bad happened, it's not your fault.

You might have heard the expression **victim blaming** before. This is what we say when a victim is blamed for something bad that happened or blames themselves. It's very wrong. The only person who should be blamed is the person who *chose* to commit the assault. Nothing any victim did, or could have done, would have stopped a perpetrator from doing it.

Victim blaming has a long history of sexism. It means that instead of hearing the message, "Men! That is *not* OK," we hear, "Women! Why did you let that happen?" Fortunately, many people are now questioning the logic of this, and global movements like #MeToo are amplifying the message.

The consent process is a series of decisions. Many of the women I see who have experienced unwanted sex are confused. It's often not clear what the moment of nonconsent is; instead, it's a series of small moments. I think it's really confusing for the person to whom it's happened because they're often not sure *what* happened. Like, "I'm not sure I 'allowed' that to happen." The thing I see very often is that people blame themselves. *Dr. Ellie Freedman*

Men can and do have their boundaries disrespected, and anyone can be assaulted by people of any gender. One of the reasons we wrote this book is that consent is an issue for everyone: men, women, trans and nonbinary people, kids and adults. No matter who you are or how you identify, you deserve support and help if something hurtful or harmful has happened—period.

Protection and support

If you take the brave step of contacting one (or more) of the below services, we suggest that you include a close friend or trusted adult in the process. If you're a close friend of someone who has been a victim, perhaps offer to support them.

If you are that close friend or trusted adult, responding with compassion is the most important thing you can do. You will have your own way of doing that, but here are some examples:

- ✸ **"I am sorry for what has happened"—which is heard as "I believe you."**

- ✸ **"What has happened is a crime"—which is heard as "This is not your fault."**

- ✸ **"I will do what I can to help"—which is heard as "You are not alone."**

Counseling services

There are specialist sexual assault counseling services for victims, even if the assault happened a while ago. Some of these are specially designed for children and young adolescents. It takes courage to talk about assault, and the good thing about specialist services is that they understand that you need to go at your own pace.

Rape, Abuse & Incest National Network (RAINN)

For telephone and online counseling and links to services in your area, call 800-656-HOPE or visit rainn.org.

Sexual assault medical care

There are specialist services for victims who have been recently assaulted and need or want medical care. Trained, caring doctors, nurses, and counselors will listen to you and offer an examination if you want one.

These services are usually located in or near a public hospital.

RAINN can give you information about your local services, and so can your local emergency department or the police. Call the number on the previous page or visit their website.

Police

Even if you're not sure whether what happened was illegal, the police should take your complaint seriously. It can help to contact them sooner rather than later so that they can investigate and collect evidence.

In an emergency, dial 911.

If you are d/Deaf or have a hearing or speech impairment, you can use a text-to-911 service, a TTY, or a relay service and the operator will connect you to the police.

If it's not an emergency, contact your local police station.

FINDING YOUR PEOPLE

In a situation where your boundaries are being disrespected, or you feel mocked, pressured, or bullied, having someone stick up for you can turn everything around. It's backup that gives you the strength to say, "Actually, no thanks. I'm not putting up with this."

ONE FRIEND CAN MAKE A WORLD OF DIFFERENCE.

Sometimes *you* need to be that friend for someone else.

As you get older, you might still want the support of your peers—but you get better at hearing their voices when they're *not* around. You might hear a familiar voice in your mind say, "Hang on, they shouldn't speak to you like that," and you know they're right! It's enough to help you push back if you need to. You also get better and more confident at standing up for yourself on your own.

Not everyone is lucky enough to have that one friend. You don't always get to choose the peer group around you when you're young. They're just the people you know at school or who live nearby. They may have rotten attitudes about consent, about people who are different from them, about sex. They may bully you, try to silence you, or mock you.

If this is where you are at, we want to say: We see you. We can be your person. If you wish you had a clearer image of the line between right and wrong, listen out for our voices in your mind. Until you find your people, we can be the ones who stand behind you, cheer you on, give you the strength you need to make the right choices.

Trust that you *will* find your people as you get older. Maybe you haven't found them yet, and that's OK. But you will. And you will champion each other, look out for each other, and love each other.

In the meantime, trust your instincts. Respect your body. Love and respect the bodies of others. And listen out for the little voice in your mind saying, "You've got this."

In power. In solidarity.

Yumi and
Dr. Melissa xx

EXPAND YOUR VOCABULARY

CONFIDENTIALITY

Keeping information private.

COERCION

Persuading someone to do something by using threats or force.

CONSENT

An agreement between people to do something together. Giving permission for someone to have or do something.

HARASSMENT

Pressure, intimidation, or offensive or tormenting behavior. Sexual harassment is unwelcome conduct of a sexual nature. It includes unwelcome sexual advances, requests for sexual favors, and other verbal, nonverbal, or physical conduct of a sexual nature.

GENDER

A person's sense of being female, male, both, neither, or something else.

MASTURBATION

Touching the genitals for sexual arousal and pleasure. It is something people can do alone and to themselves for pleasure, relaxation, and experimentation.

HORMONE

A chemical in the body made by special tissues called glands. Humans have more than fifty different hormones. Each one is a "messenger" with a specific message, sent through the bloodstream to tell another tissue to do or not do something.

PUBERTY

A whole lot of body and brain changes that usually start between eight or nine and thirteen or fourteen years of age and continue for several years. Bodies get bigger and stronger and adult sexual organs (such as breasts and genitals) develop. Brain changes lead to more problem-solving and decision-making abilities as well as possible interest in romance, sex, and intimate relationships.

PORN

Short for *pornography*, this is material (images, writing, videos, audio recordings) that is specifically designed to cause sexual arousal.

SEX

Sex can have a biological definition, based on someone's chromosomes.

The other definition refers to the behaviors and activities of a sexual nature that people engage in. This might include kissing, sexual touching, masturbation, oral sex, or sexual intercourse.

POWER

Strength, authority, or the ability to influence something that happens because of someone's social position or job.

SEXTING

Sending messages or images of a sexual nature from one person to another via text message or social media messaging.

MORE RESOURCES

CHILDHELP NATIONAL CHILD ABUSE HOTLINE

This hotline is dedicated to the prevention of child abuse of many kinds. It serves the US and Canada 24/7 and provides professional crisis counselors who can offer assistance in more than 170 languages. All contacts are confidential. You can get in touch at 1-800-4-A-CHILD or childhelphotline.org.

RAINN

Rape, Abuse & Incest National Network is America's largest anti-sexual violence organization. You can get help 24/7 at 800-656-HOPE or find resources on their website at rainn.org.

Police

Call 911 in an emergency, such as if you or another person is in danger or a crime is taking place. If you are d/Deaf or have a hearing or speech impairment, you can use a text-to-911 service, a TTY, or a relay service. For anything else, contact your local police station.

SAMHSA

SAMHSA (Substance Abuse and Mental Health Services Administration) offers a free confidential helpline that provides local referrals for people facing mental and/or substance abuse disorders. You can call them 24/7 at 800-662-HELP or visit their website at samhsa.gov for resources.

Legal Questions

The American Bar Association offers a directory of children's law programs and centers that can provide legal services to children. Find out more at www.americanbar.org/groups /litigation/committees/childrens-rights/directory/.

PFLAG

PFLAG is an organization for LGBTQ+ people, their families, and allies. For peer-to-peer support services in your community, you can contact one of the nearly four hundred PFLAG chapters across the United States. You can find them online at pflag.org.

Alcohol Basics

If you'd like to learn more about alcohol, especially as it relates to young people, visit the CDC's resources at cdc.gov/alcohol /fact-sheets.htm.

ACKNOWLEDGMENTS

This book is dedicated to all the young people who have shared their stories with me over half my life—your suffering, your joy, your losses, and your triumphs. You light up the world.

Thank you, Yumi, Marisa Pintado, and Benython Oldfield, for believing we could bring a book about consent for young people to light. Thank you to the amazing Jenny Latham, whose illustrations have brought it to life. Thanks to the rest of the incredible Hardie Grant Children's Publishing team: Pooja Desai, Luna Soo, and Penelope White.

A huge debt of gratitude goes to my expert reviewers: Georgia Carr, Jacqui Hendriks, Jane Sanders, and Peter Chown. Thanks to Renee West for sharing your insights and expert knowledge about teaching consent. And to other friends and colleagues who shared their wisdom with me: Alan McKee, Ellie Freedman, Mary Dobbie, and Tania May.

Thank you to Mitchell for all the listening and to my cheer squad: Hannah-Rose, Georgia, Samantha, and Julian. Thank you to all the wonderful young people who spoke to me about how consent figures in their lives: your names appear throughout this book, your words are sparkling gems, and your thoughts matter more than everything.

Dr. Melissa

Thank you to my friend and coauthor, Dr. Melissa Kang, who—as the writer behind Dolly Doctor—was the only medical authority kids could actually rely on to tell the truth about sexy stuff when we were younger. No question was too gooey! No moment too painful or embarrassing. Your kindness and directness in communicating were invaluable during those crucial years of childhood—not just for me but for generations of readers.

Marisa Pintado, I'm so glad we met at that party! We can joke about it, but my life changed because of that moment.

Thanks to *everyone* who works their arses off at Hardie Grant Children's Publishing, especially Penelope White, Luna Soo, Pooja Desai, and Kristy Lund-White, and to Jenny Latham for her excellent illustrations.

I owe a huge debt of gratitude to my friends who talked with me about consent over many cups of tea while I grappled with how to make this information snackable enough to maintain the attention of teenage readers while also being right and solid and useful. It was harder than it looks! So thanks to Claudine, Penny, Cass, Carla, Lisa, and Marty.

Thanks to all the teenagers who spoke to me with such candidness about their experiences. We had laughs. It was brilliant. I love you.

And biggest thanks of all goes to the parents and caregivers who have given this book to their kids. You're crucial. You're invaluable. You're doing the right thing. Thank you.

Yumi

CONTRIBUTORS

Thank you so much to our wonderful contributors:

Abby Edwards, Aimee, Professor Alan McKee, Alex, Ally Garrett, Amna Hassan, Anouk, Billy J. Russell, Casey, Professor Catharine Lumby (professor in media, gender studies researcher), Chloe, Corey, Dee Dee, Deklan Wright, Drishti, Dr. Ellie Freedman (medical director of a sexual assault service), Georgia, Hannah, Hayden Moon, Imogen Kelly, Jackson, Jacqueline Greene (treasurer of Women with Disabilities WA Inc.), Dr. Jacqui Hendriks (senior research officer and lecturer, Curtin University), Kera, Lana, Lee, Luke, Marihuzka, Marisa, Marty James, Mel Kettle, Mel Ree, Michala Banas (intimacy coordinator), Miranda, Moya, Nevo Zisin, Nick Pezza, Nicole Lee, Paula Baxter, Penelope Abdiel, Ruby, Sally Rugg, Samantha, Saxon Mullins (director of advocacy at Rape and Sexual Assault Research and Advocacy), Stella, Dr. Tania May (medical director of a sexual assault service), Tans, and Xuân.

Your honesty is so appreciated.

ABOUT THE ILLUSTRATOR

Jenny Latham is an illustrator from the United Kingdom. She has a huge passion for illustrating real people and spreading body positivity. She loves empowering people with her work and hopes it puts a smile on people's faces. Her main goal is to make people feel happy and believe they can be whoever they want to be.